GUARDIAN ANGELS

JOAN WESTER ANDERSON

GUARDIAN ANGELS

TRUE STORIES OF ANSWERED PRAYERS

LOYOLAPRESS.
A JESUIT MINISTRY
Chicago

LOYOLAPRESS.
A JESUIT MINISTRY

3441 N. Ashland Avenue
Chicago, Illinois 60657
(800) 621-1008
www.loyolapress.com

Cover design by Rick Franklin

Interior design by Adam Moroschan

Library of Congress Cataloging-in-Publication Data

Anderson, Joan Wester.
  Guardian angels : true stories of answered prayers / Joan Wester Anderson.
     p. cm.
  Includes bibliographical references.
  ISBN-13: 978-0-8294-2169-9; ISBN-10: 0-8294-2169-6
  1. Prayer—Christianity. 2. Guardian angels. 3. Angels. 4. Miracles. I. Title.
BV220.A42 2006
248.3'2—dc22
                                                      2006001222

Printed in the United States of America
16 17 18 19 20 21 22 23 Versa 13 12 11 10 9 8 7 6

CONTENTS

CONTENTS

INTRODUCTION

With hurricanes, earthquakes, fires out of control, mud slides, tornados,
flooding and severe thunderstorms tearing up the country, with the threat
of bird flu and terrorists attacks, are we sure this is a good time to take
God out of the Pledge of Allegiance?

—JAY LENO

When Hurricane Katrina roared across Florida, Louisiana, Mississippi, and Alabama in August of 2005, leaving unbelievable destruction in its wake, many people wondered if God had forgotten us and had left us unprotected. If so, why? Was this a punishment of some sort, or a warning? Or was our heavenly Father allowing us to experience, in a limited way, what life might be like without his constant care?

Such a premise is hard to accept, given our view of God as a loving Father. What parent would deliberately send pain to his children? As C. S. Lewis pointed out, "Pain is God's megaphone."

In trauma, whether personal or global, we truly refocus on what is most important. Survivors of destructive events rarely mourn the loss of a plasma-screen television or a new car. Instead, in the shocked aftermath they almost always praise God for sparing them and their loved ones. They focus on the essentials, the gifts of life and health that can never be replaced.

We might ask, then, why we can't maintain this same attitude through the ordinary times. Could it be that God has given us the blueprint for a happy life, a peaceful sojourn, in just a few biblical verses? "If my people . . . humble themselves and pray, and seek my presence and turn from their evil ways, I will hear them from heaven and pardon their sins and revive their land" (2 Chronicles 7:14).

Prayer. It must be an important activity if God holds it up as a remedy for a country's woes. It must mean that even our most generous acts of love and support for one another must be based on a foundation of prayer. Why? Prayer is the beginning, the moment in which we acknowledge our relationship with God. We put God first in our hearts. We offer him our lives, our will, our trust. Once brought into God's arms, we are energized, ready to continue our work in this life.

I suspect that the prayer God is asking of us—especially at this critical time in history—may also involve an element of risk. Perhaps simply praying in the safe confines of our homes or churches is not enough right now. Maybe we are being asked to reach out, to pray in a public manner, to acknowledge a sovereign God as our forefathers did, even to do it as a matter of course, *before* the next earthquake or hurricane heads our way. During the Mississippi river floods of 1993, one mayor announced that, "We've run out of options. There's nothing left but prayer." People of all faiths then gathered in the town square and asked God to stop the rain.

The rain continued. But for some inexplicable reason, the flooding ended. It was an awesome event, largely ignored by the media. But one wonders what might have happened if prayer had been the first option rather than the last.

One magnificent facet of prayer is that anyone can do it. From a toddler singing "Jesus Loves Me" (and didn't St. Augustine point out that "He who sings prays twice"?) to the Presidential Prayer Team, with over three million participants praying for the president's intentions every day, we all have equal access to the Father's heart. Moms In Touch International is one of many groups formed around a single theme, to protect their children from moral and physical danger. Membership can involve meeting with one or two neighbors each morning or attending a large church prayer service. There are also solitary "prayer warriors," people who feel occasionally summoned to put aside their own work or recreation and pray for a particular situation or person, even someone they've never met.

Occasionally one will also hear about a "victim soul," someone who—by suffering—is bearing burdens for others in a far higher form of prayer that most of us ever experience.

There's true power in prayer, even though we're not sure exactly how it works. Has someone ever told you, "You're in my prayers," and you actually felt that strength and comfort while you underwent a medical procedure or took a test? It happens to us all. Even hospital researchers have done studies in which some patients were prayed for (by strangers) and some with similar maladies were not; invariably the prayed-for group reported fewer surgical aftereffects and quicker release times. We have things in the right order when we pray *first*.

"I wish I could contribute some school supplies," a reader wrote me as a group of us launched a drive to help disadvantaged students. "But my budget is too tight. There's nothing I can do."

"Can you pray that these children receive what they need?" I asked her.

Of course she could, and did. And she most certainly shared in the successful results as much as if she had donated a truckload of merchandise.

Praying, of course, doesn't always bring about the results we expect. For "no" or "not yet" can be an answer to a prayer as well as "yes." God has a plan for each of us, and timing is a critical element in building our own characters and bringing this plan to fruition. As a loving Father, he must sometimes nudge us along *his* path rather than pamper us in a temporary indulgence. Nor should we expect that God's answer to a prayer will always conform to our ideas. John, an elderly gentleman in mid-Florida, was concerned about the roof on his mobile home. It was leaky and definitely needed replacement, but he had no money to do it. Instead, he prayed, informally as he had always done. "Don't forget the roof," he'd remind God at night, just before bedtime. "Whatever you decide will be fine."

Maybe John should have rephrased that, because one night a tornado swept through the area, touching down here and there. The next morning, although several of the mobile homes in John's area were spared, his was not. The entire roof was ripped off and broken into pieces. People felt sorry for John, until he smilingly reminded them that the insurance company would have to provide a new roof. Like John, perhaps our best prayers are those in which we ask God to direct our lives, when we pray for the answers that are best for us and trust that God's intense love for us will carry us through.

So this is a book about prayer. It includes angels, of course, for angels are masters at prayer. (In fact, the primary work of the highest-functioning choirs of angels is to praise and worship our God.) Angels can take our deepest yearnings, our brokenness, and our confusion to the throne of the Almighty. "See, I am sending an angel before you, to guard you on the way and to bring you to the place I have prepared," says the book of Exodus, chapter 23, verse

20. "Be attentive to him and heed his voice. . . . If you heed his voice and carry out all I tell you, I will be an enemy to your enemies and a foe to your foes." This is their purpose, these beautiful beings who have been given to us as our lifelong companions. If we don't know them already, we should make it a point to do so.

This book also includes almost all the stories first published in *Angels We Have Heard on High,* an earlier book of mine, because so many of them involved prayer. But there are new entries, too. Some of the people you'll meet recited formal prayers; others rambled incoherently at a moment of extreme stress. Some prayed for themselves; some interceded for others. Some prayers were active rather than passive. Some were prayed in solitude, while others were links in a prayer chain or were part of a religious function. The format of the prayers wasn't significant. The acknowledgement that God was in charge was all that seemed necessary.

So, may prayer become a more significant and rewarding part of your life:

- May you pray for those you love in the quiet peace of the night, and may you do it with confidence and trust.

- May you find something to celebrate about each new day, not merely those circled in red on your crowded calendar.

∞ May you greet the seasons of your heart with enthusiasm, ready to learn and love ever more deeply.

∞ May you acknowledge the pressures in your life, unburden yourself of those that can be eased, and let the angels help you carry the rest.

∞ And may you remember God's age-old promise, "I will never forsake you or abandon you" (Hebrews 13:5).

Now, let the praying begin.

PART 1

WONDERS OF PRAYER

MY SISTER, MY FRIEND

Hold a true friend with both your hands.

—NIGERIAN PROVERB

When sixteen-year-old Susan Kelly* felt blue or wanted to celebrate, she turned to music first. She and her sister Cathy, just two years younger, had had a gift for singing from the time they were toddlers growing up in Iowa. The entire extended family looked forward to get-togethers because Susan and Cathy needed no encouragement to sing for them. And when there wasn't an audience, "we harmonized around the house while doing chores," Susan says, "and to all the oldies our mom taught us," as well as hymns from the church songbooks. Both girls felt that singing had drawn them close and allowed them to avoid most of the bickering and rivalry common to many teenage sisters.

*last name changed

Now, however, Susan needed more than a song to solve her problem. She was pregnant. Her parents had been devastated at the news, especially because they did not like her boyfriend at all. But they stood by her with encouragement and helped provide a beautiful church wedding. Susan felt like a hypocrite. She had always had a close relationship with God. But now she felt he must be disappointed in her, not only for her own actions but because she had let down the family that loved her. How could God bless this union? How could she even ask?

But Cathy wouldn't accept Susan's assumptions about how God—or others—must think of her. She popped in often to give her sister a hug and a word of support. "God loves you no matter what," she reminded her sister over and over again. On good days, Susan could almost believe it.

However, there weren't very many good days. She was not long into her marriage before Susan discovered that her new husband was not as enthusiastic about impending parenthood as she was. He, too, had dropped out of school and was now working two jobs, one full-time in a factory and the other part-time at a gas station. As her due date grew closer, Susan hoped with all her heart that the baby would bridge the growing gap between them. Baby Bryan was born healthy and strong after a long and complicated labor. Susan's husband and her entire family were with her throughout it, but Cathy seemed to bring her the deepest peace and consolation, holding her hand and praying. After the birth, Susan's husband never returned to the hospital.

At home, motherhood was fascinating, scary, and amazing, all at once. Susan had planned to return to her job, but her husband was completely disinterested in the baby and would not take care of him. "I would come home, and the baby would be in the crib, wet, hungry, and screaming," she says. So she became a stay-at-home mom, and from the start, she sang to Bryan. When Cathy came to visit, she would join the song, too. Soon the girls had an entire repertoire of harmonized songs, everything from nursery rhymes to his apparent favorite, "Rock and Roll Lullaby," which never failed to put him to sleep. Susan's husband, however, was becoming more distant than ever. Susan wondered often what would become of them. Perhaps God had abandoned her after all.

When Bryan was nine months old, he developed a cold, his first real illness. By the third night, after singing countless lullabies and giving the baby one sponge bath after another, Susan was very worried. Infants' Tylenol wasn't bringing Bryan's fever down, and her husband was working late at the gas station that night, so she was alone. She had called the doctor earlier, but he had reassured her that infant colds were rarely serious, and she should relax. But now, as she felt the baby's flushed face, Susan took his temperature again. One hundred and six degrees!

"I was a little hysterical, I think," she says. "I knew I had to get Bryan to the hospital quickly, but after I strapped him into his car seat and roared off, I realized I should get his father, too. So I drove to the gas station first." But when she got there, she saw her husband standing outside the station, kissing a young woman.

This discovery was too shocking and huge to deal with just then, so Susan shot out of the gas station lot and sped down the highway. By the time she reached the hospital emergency room, Bryan was having trouble breathing, and his fever had spiked to one hundred and eight. Dehydration had set in. When the nurses started an IV in each arm, he didn't even move.

Susan sat, exhausted and terrified, outside the intensive care unit, watching through the window at the nurses' station as the baby's chest barely moved. "Please God, save him, save him" was all she could say. At some point, her family members came, except for Cathy, who was too young to visit the ICU. Susan's husband also arrived. She couldn't think of anything to say to him—everything seemed vague, as if she were in some kind of fog. All that mattered to her was Bryan.

But would God answer her prayer? Was he still disappointed in her? Finally, with the nurses' consent, Susan climbed into the oxygen tent, lay on the bed beside Bryan, clutched his little hand, and continued to pray. But after five hours and several bags of fluids, his temperature had dropped only a degree. The doctor told everyone to go home, and everyone did, except Susan. "There has to be something I can do," she begged the nurse on duty. "Anything."

"Well . . ." The nurse looked around and then quickly left the room. She returned with a pitcher of cool water and a syringe with the needle detached. "Fill the syringe with the water from the pitcher," the nurse instructed Susan, "and slowly drip the water down the baby's throat."

Susan got back under the tent and lifted Bryan into her arms. She would do this. She *had* to! Somehow she knew it was Bryan's last chance. But it was so hard to reach the pitcher, then dip and fill the syringe with the baby in her arms. Susan struggled to balance everything, but the water dribbled out of Bryan's mouth. She was so intent on her tasks that when the nurse came back, Susan didn't look up.

"Here, let me fill the syringe and hand it to you," a woman said. But it wasn't the nurse. It was Cathy!

"Oh, Cathy, I'm so glad you're here!" Susan's eyes filled with tears. How had her sister managed to sneak in, despite being under-age? And wasn't it awfully late? Who had driven her? But this was not the time for questions. Calmly, Cathy bent over the pitcher and filled the syringe, handing it to Susan, then taking it back to refill it. The baby settled down, swallowing each drop with his eyes still closed. Peace—in this unlikely and desperate place—began to move across Susan's heart, banishing her terrible fear. She wasn't alone anymore.

Softly she began to sing Bryan's favorite, "Rock and Roll Lullaby." Within seconds, Cathy's voice joined hers, easily harmonizing as they had always done. From "Lullaby" they moved to other favorites as they rhythmically passed the syringe back and forth. No conversation was necessary.

An hour passed, then Bryan fell asleep. Almost immediately the nurse came in the room to check him. "His fever has broken," she smiled at Susan. "That's good news."

Susan looked for Cathy, but she had apparently slipped out of the room. Exhausted and relieved, her hand cramped, Susan lay back on the bed.

For three more days, Susan stayed at Bryan's bedside. Her husband visited, too, but both of them knew now that their marriage had ended. Separating was the right decision, but Susan couldn't help but feel sorrowful. Once again, she had failed at something important. God must be so dissatisfied with her.

Finally, Bryan was discharged, and Susan drove with him to her family's home. Cathy was waiting at the door to greet her. "Oh Cathy . . ." Susan hugged her. "Thank you so much for coming to the hospital that night! You were wonderful!"

Cathy hugged her, then stepped back, a puzzled look on her face. "What are you talking about, Sue? I was never at the hospital. You know I'm not old enough to visit the ICU."

Had it been a dream? No! Susan had taken the syringe home with her, and would never forget it passing between them, holding those tiny drops of lifesaving water. She remembered how cramped her own hand had been. But she would say no more until she had visited the hospital staff to thank them for their care.

A few days later, she did, and the same ICU nurse took her aside. "I'll always remember how you stayed up all night alone with your son, singing the whole time," the nurse said.

"But I wasn't alone," Susan pointed out. "Don't you remember the younger girl, the one that sang with me?"

"There wasn't anyone with you," the nurse insisted. "I could see you clearly through the window, dropping the water into the baby's mouth. You were the only one in the room."

Suddenly, as if a warm blanket was settling around her, Susan understood. Cathy had been right all along. God loved her now, and had always loved her, just as she loved her baby. It was he, her Eternal Parent, who had arranged for an angel to watch with her that night in the hospital. Not just any angel either, but one who resembled the person Susan had always been able to trust and depend upon most: her sister.

Susan went on to become a much-cherished wife and the mother of five children. Like all of us, she has encountered trouble and disappointment along the way. But she has never doubted God's forgiveness. And, whenever they can, she and Cathy sing praises to him.

FAITH IN THE FIRE

When we dream, the soul transcends the limits of the body,
and holds divine communication with the angels.

—St. Athanasius

When Carolyn Shafer moved to Tempe, Arizona, as a young mother, she had never heard of intercessory prayer, that is, praying specifically for another person's needs. But she wanted the companionship of other women, so she joined a Bible-study group at a nearby Methodist church. "We were all pretty uninformed about God and spiritual faith," she says. "We had no idea how powerful prayer could be."

In the middle of one night, Carolyn was startled into wakefulness. "I had a strong conviction that something bad was happening to Jackie, one of the women in our group. I knew her only slightly, but someone had mentioned that she had bronchitis." Was that the problem? And what should Carolyn do about it? Phone Jackie? This late? Surely the woman had a family to rely on. And wouldn't it be embarrassing to awaken Jackie and discover that this strange feeling was only Carolyn's imagination?

Carolyn plumped her pillows. She would forget it and go back to sleep. But the unease persisted. "Because I didn't know what else to do, I finally began to pray for Jackie. Again and again I implored God to protect her from whatever was wrong." Gradually, the urgency disappeared, and Carolyn finally fell asleep.

The following morning, Carolyn was still puzzling about the episode. Jackie would probably think she was odd, but she needed to touch base. "Good morning," she said, smiling as Jackie answered the doorbell. "I just came by to ask . . . well . . . did anything happen to you last night?"

"Last night?"

"Yes. Were you in trouble, or sick?"

Jackie looked astonished. "How did you know? My bronchitis flared up—it was the worst attack I've ever had. I was gasping for air and trying to wake my husband to take me to the hospital. But all of a sudden, everything seemed to calm down."

The women looked at each other. "I was praying for you," Carolyn admitted. "I think God woke me and told me to do it." She almost expected Jackie to laugh at her.

But Jackie's eyes were filling with tears. "Would God do that for me?" she asked.

Then she confessed to Carolyn that she had been wrestling with a quiet fear that God didn't really care about her. But this tender gesture, brought to her from someone she barely knew was all the reassurance she needed.

"We went on to become the dearest of friends," Carolyn says today. "God can use anyone to touch another, if we're willing."

Intercessory prayer, as Carolyn discovered, is very powerful. We are all intercessors when we pray for one another, even when there's no emergency involved. (And it appears that angels often intercede for us, too.) But intercessory prayer can also be a specific ministry to which a person is compelled on occasion. Such people are rarely willing, nor do they consider themselves worthy of such a daunting task. But it is just that willingness to serve, despite feelings of inadequacy, that graces the plans of God.

The fire call came in on April 3, 1995, at about 1:00 a.m. A blaze in a two-story apartment building. *Fairly routine,* thought firefighter Paul Grams, of Rockford, Illinois. He and his partners, Ron and John, were the first to arrive on the scene.

The first floor was unoccupied, the firefighters learned from neighbors who were gathering to watch the drama. But then a bystander ran up. "I think there are people living upstairs!" he shouted. "A lady and her little grandchild."

Possible victims! The scenario shifted as the three men raced into the building. "The smoke was so thick that it blocked any light, and even muffled sound," Paul relates. "We searched the apartment, but we couldn't find anyone." The atmosphere seemed strange, even surreal, as they crawled around in darkness. Paul bumped into someone. "John, is that you?" he asked.

But there was no answer. "Ron?" Paul questioned. Again, no response. But the presence had been moving, not lying still like someone overcome by smoke. Who was it?

Again, Paul crawled along, feeling his way. Long minutes passed. Once more, he bumped into something right in front of him. Had other firefighters come into the apartment without the three men knowing it? "Who is this?" Paul demanded.

"You will never get out of here alive." The menacing message emanated from whatever was in front of him. It was not in audible words, but somehow it permeated his spirit, bringing fear and peril into the murkiness. "John!" Paul called again. "Is that you?"

No one answered. Paul felt terribly alone. Something was wrong. They had been crawling for almost fifteen minutes, and their air supply would soon be exhausted. But where was the exit? The smoke was even denser than before, and nothing could be seen in this heavy gray fog. A chill went through Paul as he realized that he and his companions were lost.

"You'll never get out of here alive." Again the threatening words came. Paul's skin prickled. Although he couldn't see anyone speaking, he recognized the voice now. It was Evil.

Sherry Zahorik, of nearby Machesney Park, Illinois, was having a dream. She was in a room, a foggy room. Three people were crawling in front of her, frantically searching for something. Sherry felt as though she were in their midst, watching them go through this terrible assignment. She could feel their confusion, and something more as well. "There was a terrible demonic presence permeating the room," she says. "Whenever one of these people would bump into something and call the name of his friend, this presence would laugh. And it would say, 'You will never get out of here alive.'"

Abruptly, Sherry awakened, sat up, and peered at her alarm clock. Just a little past 1:00 a.m. Her chest felt heavy, as if a huge weight was lying on it, and she could hardly breathe. Sherry blinked. She was definitely awake. Yet it seemed as if she was still in the dream. "I knew in an instant that I should start praying."

Every now and then, Sherry is awakened by an urge to intercede for someone. On the face of it, the impulse seems a bit strange. She doesn't know exactly what the situation is about or who she is praying for. And why, she has often wondered, should *she* be tapped for this job? Surely her prayers are no more powerful than anyone else's.

However, Sherry wants to be obedient to God whenever he calls on her. And so, despite her questions and her fatigue, she prays.

Tonight, however, the circumstances were different. As Sherry began to pray, she continued to be aware of her dream and the scenario it had presented. Perhaps this time God was showing her something *specific* so her prayers could be more focused. "Oh God," Sherry began. "You know where these people are. Save them, Lord. Remove them from this danger . . ."

It seemed to Paul as if he had been crawling in this blackness forever. Where were the others? Although he couldn't see anything, Paul heard Ron calling the chief on his radio. "Ladder Company Number One is lost on the second floor! Someone needs to ventilate the building immediately, so we can find our way out!"

"Ron!" Paul called. "Where are you?"

"Over here!" Ron sounded far away. But as Paul attempted to crawl toward him, he bumped into the presence again. It was laughing, a sneering, depraved sound. "You will never get out of here alive," it said.

Where was the chief's answering radio transmission? Where was the sound of glass breaking as other firefighters smashed windows to remove some of the smoke? Paul strained to hear, but there was no sound at all. An image came to him, photos that had accompanied a recent article in a firefighter magazine. "It was about a firefighter who had gotten lost in a smoky room and died when he ran out of air," Paul says. "The pictures showed handprints in the soot on the wall, where he had searched in vain for the window—which was just inches away." Would their deaths be written about in a similar way?

Paul heard a faint warning bell. It sounded like John's air tank, out of air. Was John already lying unconscious on the floor? Obviously, the chief hadn't received Ron's message. Paul grabbed his own radio. "Chief, where are you? We're trapped on the second floor; we're lost in the smoke and almost out of air. Break out the windows!" But no answer came. Except the now-familiar whisper of the gloating presence in the room. "You'll never get out," it said, "never, never . . ."

An hour had passed. Assuming that her prayer time wouldn't last too long, Sherry had begun while lying in bed. But each time she tried to finish and fall asleep, she'd felt the same weight on her chest, so heavy that she could neither sleep nor even easily breathe. So she was now in the living room.

Her husband had come out to check on her. "Are you all right?" He was used to her night vigils, and was himself an intercessor, but this situation was lasting an unusually long time.

Oh, how she wanted the comfort of her bed, and sleep. But God had not released Sherry yet. She knew he was telling her something. The Lord of the Universe, the All-Powerful One, still requested her effort, her love and sacrifice poured out for others in his family, even though she didn't know who they were. Standing in God's presence on behalf of someone who needed help—that was what being a prayer warrior was all about. If she was called to this work, she didn't need to understand the "why" of it. Only obedience was required.

Nor did she understand the role of demonic presence in this terrible event. While praying, she had sensed a vision of firefighters, one of them clawing blindly at a wall, thinking it was a window. They were in mortal danger, both physically and spiritually, and it would take strong prayers to save them. "I need to keep going," she told her husband. He nodded and went back to bed.

Help would come. It had to. But as he waited for an answer to his radio call, Paul quietly resigned himself to his death, and Ron's and John's, too. What a tragedy for the engine company, for all the families and friends involved, especially his youngest daughter, who would turn thirteen tomorrow. But if it was God's will, then maybe death was inevitable. Paul remembered the voice's sinister whisper: "Never, never . . ."

Suddenly, as if a cool refreshing wind was blowing through the room, Paul knew that the voice was wrong. Someone somewhere was wrestling with this evil presence, doing battle for him and his buddies. Someone was covering him with prayer power, sending reassurance and hope. He felt it, in the most tangible way. Peace filled him.

Seconds later, John, now completely out of air, found a window and broke it out with both hands. Firefighters on the ground placed a ladder to the window, and John scrambled to safety. Paul and Ron were next, their tanks barely functioning. On the ground, the men filled their lungs with clean pure air and related what had happened, including the mix-up over the messages. No tenants had been home on the second floor, they were told, nor had other firefighters come to the apartment.

Relieved, the men went back to their work. Later, however, as Paul stood in three feet of water in the basement, he again felt a sense of danger. Looking up, he saw the charred joists, the huge sections of floor burned completely through, and realized that everything could collapse at any moment, trapping him yet again. *I've faced enough hazards for one night,* he thought as he clambered up the basement stairs. Whoever was praying for him must still be on duty. He glanced at his watch: it was almost 5:00 a.m. He should call his wife, Val, before she left for her secretarial job at Rockford's Christian Life Center School, and tell her not to worry if she heard about the fire on the morning news.

Sherry was exhausted. Long ago, she had run out of words, and was now praying in tongues, a wordless plea arising from somewhere deep in her soul. The evil presence was still there, she knew. And, although she no longer envisioned the firefighters crawling in smoke, she knew they were still depending on her. She wouldn't weaken, she told herself. She would go on, as long as necessary, because God had asked her to.

Then, unexpectedly, Sherry felt a lift within her spirit. "It was like something being released," she says. "The situation was over, everything was all right, and I was no longer needed." She would probably never know what had happened. But perhaps she could catch a brief nap before going to her job at Rockford's Christian Life Center School. She crawled into bed, glancing at her clock. It was just before five.

What a hectic day! School secretary Val Grams hadn't had a chance to tell coworkers about her husband's ordeal at the fire. But between phone calls and office details, she continued to give silent thanks to God for sparing Paul and the others. It had been such a close call.

At one point, Val thought she heard Sherry Zahorik, one of the day-care workers, telling the principal about being up half the night praying for some people in a fire. Val knew Sherry only slightly, and Sherry had never met Paul, didn't even know he was a firefighter. What a strange coincidence.

It was not until the school day was over that Val had a chance to go out to the playground and ask Sherry to tell her the story. Only then, through their tears, did both women realize what God had done.

Paul Grams and Sherry Zahorik never determined the reason for the evil presence in the burning building that night. Perhaps the site had been used for witchcraft or occult purposes, and spirits continued to linger. Nor do they understand fully how prayer works, how it protects others, or why God chooses to communicate through dreams. The link Paul and Sherry shared on one fateful night remains a mystery now, and may be one forever. But they are grateful. And they believe.

The Welcome Visitor

It was first whispered among the seraphim and cherubim,
and then said aloud among the angels and archangels,
that he didn't even look like an angel!

—CHARLES TAZEWELL, *THE LITTLEST ANGEL*

About twenty-five years ago, Dr. Clyta Harris and her husband separated. Clyta was left with three young children and a fourth on the way. "I was devastated and so lonely I was physically ill," she says. "I was in a graduate program, working full time, and trying to provide a secure home for my little ones."

Due to financial problems, Clyta had sold their nice, large house and purchased a smaller, not-so-nice one that she could afford on her salary. When the weather got colder that year, a family of mice moved in, plaguing Clyta and the children. Clyta was brave most of the time, but the sight of a mouse sprinting across her living room floor reduced her to a bowl of mush. One evening she awakened her oldest son at 3:00 a.m. to help her find a mouse—she could hear it scratching but could not locate it. Her son found it in a small waste-basket, anxiously trying to climb the slick sides and run for safety. "Another night I awoke, and in the light from a street lamp saw a mouse sitting on my big toe on top of the covers," Clyta recalls. "I kicked as hard as I could, and I never did know where that little critter landed." Once, Clyta went into her living room just after dark and surprised not one but five baby mice scurrying across the floor.

Clyta panicked. "I had known almost all my life that God cared for me, but I had never thought to ask him for help with this problem." Frustrated beyond imagination, she raised her voice and her hands toward heaven and implored, "Oh, God, please help me with this mouse problem!" She wasn't sure she really believed God would. Within minutes of that plea, the doorbell rang. It was a student who had arranged to drop off a research paper Clyta was going to type for him (one of her many part-time jobs). As she opened the door to let him in, a large white and black cat moved stealthily around the door and into her living room. The student seemed as surprised as Clyta was at the sight of the animal. Had it been hanging around her door, waiting for it to open? How odd, even amazing, that a cat had appeared almost immediately after she had prayed.

"Kitty cat," Clyta spoke to her, "are you the answer to my prayer about the mouse problem?" She had never allowed an animal to stay in her house, but it was a cold night, so she let the cat stay in the garage. "The next morning I let her out, and she went on her way.

"The following evening I heard her meowing outside the front door. Once again she spent the night in my garage. This happened daily for about two weeks."

Clyta noticed that the cat was not especially affectionate or playful with her or the children. On the contrary, it seemed to be on a mission and, although it would accept a saucer of warm milk occasionally, it was otherwise completely focused on the presumed task.

The furry visitor arrived each evening like clockwork. And then, one night, the cat did not appear. Amazingly, neither did the mice! "We never spotted another sign of a mouse in the two years we lived in that house," Clyta says. "Nor did we ever see our angel cat again."

Did God really send that cat? Was she an angel in disguise, sent to answer Clyta's prayer? "Did God know that in my time of weakness I needed him to show me how much he cared for even my 'small' problems? I believe the answer to all those questions is a resounding Yes! God knows and cares and meets our needs, sometimes in the most unexpected ways."*

*In fact, Clyta and her husband reunited, and will celebrate their fortieth wedding anniversary next year.

MARLENE'S MINISTRY

Never doubt that a small group of committed people can change the world. Indeed, it is the only thing that ever has.
—MARGARET MEAD

A s we have seen, prayer, whether for ourselves or intercessory, has real power, and everyone should belong to a group that can pray together. One of the largest prayer chains on the Internet, www.prayervine.org, was started by Marlene JuHaros, whose own story is an inspiring one.

After Marlene converted to Christianity many years ago, she met a minister and his wife who needed a place to stay. Marlene invited them to share her large house in Scottsdale, Arizona, rent free. The three of them decided to hold a Bible-study group on Friday and Saturday nights, hoping that a few street kids in their area might attend. One thing led to another (as it so often does when God is doing the leading), "and before I knew it, I had let a couple of homeless young women move in," Marlene recalls. "The Bible nights attracted about fifty young people, many of them drug addicts and runaways, most of them homeless and troubled. We took many of them in until every vacant spot in the house was filled." Marlene named the ministry Harbor House.

It took faith to do this work of mercy, and Marlene is convinced that faith in God can be as natural as breathing. However it isn't until we begin trusting God that such faith is activated. "As long as I could do it myself, I didn't look to God to do it," Marlene explains. But once her savings were gone and she was in real need, it wasn't long before she began asking for mini-miracles—every day.

The young people were grateful for the shelter and the warmth of Marlene's welcome, and they obeyed the few rules she insisted upon—no drugs, no alcohol, and everyone sharing the chores. "We didn't even require them to attend Bible study and prayer meetings, because I felt that the Holy Spirit had to move upon them before they would have the desire to change." Marlene says.

The praying irritated a young biker named Freddie. One day, as the prayer meeting began, Freddie started mowing the lawn. Then he stomped into the house, picked up the telephone book, and started reading out names, with a mock prayer for each. People just went on praying. "By the time the meeting was over, Freddie had given his life to God and was a changed man," Marlene recalls. "Little did we know that Freddie had escaped from Folsom Prison. He turned himself in after that." Eventually, Harbor House received a letter from Freddie. He had started a prayer group at Folsom, and they had just held their first all-night prayer vigil. Freddie went on to lead many prisoners to Christ. (In fact, according to Marlene, more than 300 young adults who spent time at Harbor House became Christians, and many went on to become ministers.)

Although there were numerous challenges in living with that many young adults, perhaps the most difficult for Marlene was feeding a crowd of at least thirty every evening. There were no outside sponsors to ask, no organizations set up to help. Marlene let the neighborhood grocers know of her need in case they had any leftovers, but the responsibility was hers.

"We lived on faith," she says. "I taught the girls how to cook, and also to 'pray in the food,' or the money to buy the food for all these appetites." Amazingly, it always worked. There was never a time when the cupboards were completely empty—although there were a lot of close calls. Young Marla, the first girl to move in with Marlene, realized at about 5:00 p.m. one day that it was her turn to provide the food. Marla had been so busy ministering to people that day that she had forgotten. She grabbed Marlene and a few others to pray. "Lord," she began, "I was busy doing your work today. Can you send someone with food for tonight, already cooked?"

This was getting pretty specific, and Marlene admits her own faith wasn't as strong as Marla's was right then. But the women continued to pray, and at five-thirty the doorbell rang. A man they didn't know was standing there, holding huge buckets of Kentucky Fried Chicken, with all the trimmings. He had been on his way home from work, he explained, when God spoke to him, asking him to buy food for the kids at Harbor House.

On another day, it was Marlene's turn to pray and to make dinner that evening. The kitchen was completely bare, so Marlene started with prayer the first thing that morning. "As I prayed and asked God what to fix, I was confident that I heard 'fried chicken, potatoes, broccoli, and strawberry pie,'" she says. Almost immediately the phone rang. It was the local grocery store, letting Marlene know that an anonymous donor had just come in and purchased six chickens for Harbor House. Marlene was pleased; God was obviously answering her prayer and would certainly supply everything for the evening meal.

Her faith was strengthened when potatoes and broccoli arrived in the daily box of vegetables that another supermarket saved for them from produce taken off the shelves. Nothing left now to "pray in" except the pies. Confidently, Marlene baked the crusts.

At about four-thirty however, she became a little concerned. No strawberries (or any money to buy them) had yet arrived. Marlene had a dollar, so she asked one of the young men to go to a nearby fruit market and buy as many strawberries as the dollar would provide. Just a few moments later, he called her. "A pint of strawberries costs $1.49," he reported.

Disappointed, Marlene told him to come home, and went back to the prayer room. "God," she began, "I already told everyone that you were going to supply our strawberry pies. They're going to lose faith in my judgment if you don't."

The Lord interrupted. "Oh ye of little faith."

Marlene stopped. She should be praising and thanking God for whatever he was about to do, praying in the food as she had taught the others to do, not complaining. And so she did, until she heard the young man she had sent to the fruit market. He was in the kitchen, calling to her.

What now? Marlene went to the kitchen. There on the table was a large battered crate. "I was following a truck on the way home, and a box fell out of it," the beaming young man explained. "The truck kept on going, but I stopped to get the box out of the street so no one would hit it. Look what was inside!"

Marlene already knew. Not one pint, but twenty-four pints of fresh, plump, and (as everyone discovered at dinner) the most delicious strawberries they'd ever tasted. "My God will fully supply whatever you need . . ." (Philippians 4:19). It was a wonderful meal.

"There were many miracles there," Marlene says. "Once we see that God does hear and that he does answer, faith becomes second nature. Yes, having faith is difficult at times, but the more prayers God answers for us, I suppose the more we expect him to do so."

One of the neighbors who had been a faithful attendee at the Friday night Bible studies was Steve JuHaros. He had recently returned home from a stint in the marines and was living with his mother, about a block away. During the next months, seeing what Harbor House was trying to accomplish, he began collecting food for the residents. He and Marlene were the perfect couple, and by the time the minister and his wife had decided to move on, Steve and Marlene were engaged to be married. Of all the men in the world, Marlene was convinced she'd found the only one willing to help her keep Harbor House open. "How are you going to manage?" friends asked her. "If you and Steve are both working in the ministry, how will your bills get paid?"

From time to time Marlene thought about that, too. But she had lived these past years with prayer and faith as her support system, and God had never failed her. Yet it would be nice if he sent her a sign. As the wedding date approached, however, no miracles occurred.

Marlene had dreamed of an elaborate wedding. Financially, of course, it was out of the question. So the couple decided to elope. "Some friends made arrangements with their local pastor to marry us," Marlene says, "so that afternoon there were just the five of us in church."

Marlene and Steve were standing in front of the pastor, ready to recite their vows, when Steve felt an overwhelming feeling of regret. "Lord," he prayed silently, "Marlene loves people so much, and she has so many friends. They should all be here today. I wish I could have given her that kind of wedding."

Steve, turn around. Steve heard the unmistakable command in his heart. Turn around to a deserted church? He wouldn't. But the little push came again, and reluctantly Steve obeyed. Amazed at what he saw, he began to sob.

For the church wasn't empty at all. From one wall to the other, and from front to back, every pew was filled with angels. Each of them was dressed in what appeared to be their Sunday best—beautiful white garments trimmed in gold. There was an air of excitement about them. Many were good-naturedly pushing each other aside so they could see better, while others jostled for positions in the very first pews.

In the center of the angels, Steve saw a bright light shining down on Jesus, who stood in their midst. Why was the Lord so far back in the crowd? Steve wondered with part of his mind, while the other part registered astonishment and incredulity at the scene. Slowly the thought came to him that Jesus could certainly see everything no matter where he stood, and Jesus wanted Steve to be able to see *him,* to know absolutely that he was there, witnessing this special occasion. For this reason, Jesus was allowing the front row view to the angels.

Meanwhile, Marlene had noticed that Steve was crying. "I thought, *He is either taking this* very seriously *or he's changed his mind and doesn't know how to tell me.*" But when the ceremony began, Steve was as attentive as any bridegroom. His eyes filled with tears again several times—especially when the angels in the front came even closer, almost gathering around the little knot of people. It wasn't until that evening that Steve was able to share his vision with his bride.

Marlene and Steve would go on to attend Western Bible Institute, develop a kids' crusade and a television series, and grapple with health problems. Marlene would form a prayer network, which has been in existence for eleven years and has over twelve hundred branches, each with groups of their own, ranging from five members to five thousand. (When a request is posted at the Web site, many from all around the world can be praying immediately.)

All of these future events were hidden from their eyes when the angels came to attend their wedding. (And perhaps, as with all couples, that is a blessing.) But it was certainly a sign for Marlene. "I've never once doubted that Steve was the man that I was supposed to marry. And I've never once wished that I had any other wedding than the one the Lord organized for us."

SHIELD US, OH ANGELS

(S)he who has learned to pray has learned the greatest secret
of a holy and happy life.

—WILLIAM LAW

It was a hot July day in 2003, and Susan Archie was in her back-yard, looking at the big tractor her husband used when he cut the lawn. He had always promised to teach her how to drive it, but with all the outside chores at their rural home in South Carolina, he hadn't gotten around to it yet. Right now he was working in front, but the back lawn needed cutting, and the tractor didn't look all that hard to drive. She did know how to stop and go, and it would be one less chore for him if she just did it.

She checked on her six-year-old son, Joshua, who was riding an old lawn mower that his dad had adjusted to go very slowly, so Joshua wouldn't get hurt. He was enthralled with all things mechanical and probably knew more about the tractor than Susan did. "Stay over there, Joshua," she called to him. "I'm going to cut the grass on this side."

She climbed up and onto the seat before she had time to reconsider. The wheels on the tractor were up to her nose, and the cutting blade was seven feet long. It all looked potentially lethal, but she wouldn't think about any of that. Plenty of women drove tractors. She turned on the ignition, and the engine sprang to life.

One pass along the outer edge of the grass, a turn, and then another pass. Susan was doing just fine. Joshua had approached once, yelling something, but she couldn't hear him and had waved him away. Now he was back on the safe side of the lawn. Or was he? Suddenly, Susan realized that Joshua was not where she'd thought he was. Frantically she looked around. There he was, off the little lawn mower, running right alongside her! "Joshua, get away!" Susan stepped on the brakes.

"Mom, you're not cutting it right!" she heard him shout. Then Joshua attempted to jump onto the tractor. In a horrified moment, Susan's feet came off the pedals, throwing Joshua off. He slid beneath the tractor, and the huge wheel rolled over—and stopped—on his stomach and chest. She could only see his head, sticking out from beneath the machine. "Joshua!" Susan screamed, trying to turn off the engine. Her husband came running from the front yard. "He's under the wheel! I've killed him!" Susan leaped off as her husband cut the tractor's power. Both parents rushed to Joshua. As if in a dream, Susan noticed that her son was now lying on his side, with the wheel off of him, and he had somehow avoided the blade. "I'll get him out!" Susan's husband said. She ran for the phone in the house.

The shock of the unbelievable scene stayed with her as she phoned the paramedics. Why hadn't she been more careful? The wheel could have cut off his air supply—and had the blade done damage she hadn't yet seen? *God, God . . .* Her heart seemed ready to burst.

Since the Archies lived so far into the country, rather than wasting precious time giving the paramedics directions, Susan asked them to meet her and Joshua at a country store several miles away. She ran back to the yard. Her husband had somehow gotten Joshua out from under the tractor, and he was lying on the ground. Susan realized that the six year old was conscious and breathing, and there was no sign that he had been cut by the blade. "I'm okay, Daddy, it doesn't hurt," Joshua was protesting.

"Lie still, Joshua, and don't talk," the adults told him as they carefully carried him to the truck. *He couldn't be okay,* Susan thought. She had felt the huge wheel go over him. His lungs must be crushed, and she didn't want to think about what internal injuries he might have. Would Joshua die because she hadn't learned to drive the tractor? From her cell phone, she again called 911 to update the ambulance, and then called her mother to alert her church's prayer chain.

Word immediately went out over the hills and hamlets. There was power in prayer. But could it save Joshua's life?

The truck sped down the country road. Before they even reached the store, Susan saw the paramedics pull up. They had apparently decided to airlift Joshua to a larger hospital, because the Lifeflight helicopter set down in the parking lot just a few minutes later. Susan and her husband would have to drive, since there wasn't room in the helicopter for them. "As they were getting ready to put Joshua in the helicopter, I kissed him and told him that I loved him," Susan says. "He told me again that he was okay." She watched the plane take off, asking angels to encircle it. Then, as she and her husband pulled out of the parking lot, Susan noticed that the lot was almost full of people—people she knew, and some she didn't, all alerted to Joshua's condition. They had come to the store to offer silent support, just to let her know they were praying.

Susan prayed all the way to the hospital. And when they finally entered the emergency room, the first voice she heard was her son's. "My mama wasn't cutting the grass right," he was explaining to someone.

"That's Joshua!" she shouted. "Where is he?"

Physicians checked every inch of Joshua, and ran several scans. They discovered that his liver had been practically cut in two, his lungs were bruised, and two ribs were cracked. Yet, aside from bloodshot eyes due to the pressure of the tractor, Joshua looked fine. It was unbelievable that he did not have more serious injuries. And he wasn't in any pain. "I want to go home, Mom," he kept telling Susan. "I feel fine, honest." A very lucky little boy.

Yet Susan knew it was far more than luck. From the moment she had asked for prayers, they had come. The first gathering in the parking lot led to visits at the hospital, people dropping off notes at her house and phoning the hospital, leaving messages of hope. Others wrote letters from faraway places, people of all faiths, all assuring her that they were praying for her son's healing. Again, she remembered the moment of the accident, and her bewilderment that Joshua had been run over while lying on his back, and yet when she reached him, he was on his side, with the wheel completely off.

"He seemed completely normal," Susan says. "Despite his IV, he was hungry, and after the first night, he actually roamed the hospital halls looking for something to do." The liver mended without surgery.

Joshua went home in less than a week and has had no ill effects. One night shortly after his release from the hospital, he and Susan were talking about the accident. "Did it hurt when the tractor ran over you?" she asked.

"I didn't feel it run over me," Joshua says. "God was with me."

God, and a team of angels to lift the wheel. Susan firmly believes that there is power in prayer.

Judy Trevino tossed and turned. This flu was *so* uncomfortable. For days, she and her two children, Justin and Jamie, ages six and four, had been in bed in the family's mobile home, waiting for the sickness to lift. Although it was spring, the past few weeks had been unseasonably hot, and a strong wind whirled the dry earth and whipped the tall grass, adding to everyone's distress. They needed rain in this south Texas land, needed it bad. Even the cows seemed surly, grazing fitfully and lowing more than usual.

Judy was aware of it all, but in a distracted way. Her husband was away on business, and if it weren't for her mother, Mary, who lived in another trailer on their property, she'd be in real trouble. As it was, all she could do was use this enforced downtime to catch up on her praying—and ask heaven for relief from it all.

Her parents had purchased these fifty acres in the late seventies to live on and to breed cattle. Her brother-in-law eventually added a herd, too. After she and Joe married and lived away for a while, they purchased their own mobile home and set it up on the family property. Her father had died a few years ago, but Joe and his brother were able to keep things running.

Now, Judy was dozing off again when she heard the trailer door open. Looking up, she saw her mother's worried face. "A big grass fire!" Mary announced. "It's heading this way! Help me wet down the yard and houses!"

Judy sat up and grabbed for her shoes. Until now, a grass fire had never come close to them, but Judy knew they were fairly common, especially during droughts. Fires could be devastating, consuming everything, even leaping across roads. Worse, farms here were served by volunteer firefighters, who—because of the distances—weren't always available immediately. Right now, Judy and Mary were the only line of defense.

The women ran outside to get the hose, but it was already too late. Smoke hung thick in the air, and flames snapped and popped. An orange wall, resembling ocean waves, rolled across the fields towards them. "Mom, it's jumped the road!" Judy cried. The inferno, pushed by the fierce wind, was indeed already on their property, licking the fence posts, greedily consuming everything in its path. The barn would surely go. And the cows! But it was too late to risk saving them—they were grazing far beyond the trailers, out of reach even if the women had time. Horrified, Judy realized that the fire was almost upon them! "Mom, get the kids!" she called over the noise of the flames. "I'll get the car!"

Her heart pounding, Judy raced to the car, got it started, and pulled up alongside the trailer door. Her mother staggered outside with the drowsy children, dragged them and Pepe her Chihuahua into the backseat, and leapt into the front seat. Judy tore along the sandy lane toward the gate, a mile away, seemingly in a race with the fire. It was hot, so hot! Judy wiped the sweat from her face. They were actually *in* the fire now! Were they going to escape? Only God could save them now. *God and his angels . . .*

A fire truck bearing volunteers shot past them. A welcome sight, but the men would need more help. *Oh, angels . . .* Judy couldn't find the words. Soon, the fire was behind them and the smoke thinned. Judy pulled in the drive at a friend's house several miles away and quickly called Joe to report the situation. Only then, talking to her husband, did she begin to comprehend the enormity of what was happening. The trailers, the outbuildings, their livestock and crops—all were probably destroyed by now. And if not, it was only a matter of time. There was the propane tank sitting behind their homes, next to an old pickup. Once a spark touched that tank, an explosion was inevitable. They were going to lose everything.

Mary refused to believe it. She called her other daughter. "Start a prayer chain," she directed. "Pray for us and our neighbors and the firefighters. Ask God for a force stronger than nature. Ask him for a wall of angels to protect everything!" Judy realized that her mother was asking for a miracle. But wasn't that the only thing that could save them?

At least five hours had passed before one of the volunteers came back, covered with soot and sweat. He reported that several hundred acres had burned, and at least seven rural fire departments had been involved. But the fire was out, and no one had been hurt. Everyone could go home now. Judy caught her mother's eye. "Is everything gone?" she asked the firefighter.

Instead of answering, he smiled wearily. "Just go take a look," he said.

That didn't sound good. Slowly, Judy got back into the car. "We're okay," she reassured her frightened children. "That's the most important thing." But even though she really believed that, she wondered how they would start life all over again.

Judy reached the gate and saw Joe waiting for her. He had arrived just ahead of her and the firefighters had kept him away until now. Slowly, everyone went down the lane. The smell of smoke was everywhere, and acres of blackened grass lay where, that morning, all had been green. A few tongues of fire still flickered on the ground, and smoke rose from the scorched fence posts. *It must all be gone,* Judy thought. But she drove a bit farther. Then Justin pointed. "Look, Mommy!" he shouted. "Our house!"

Both trailers stood safe and sound. "No burned paint!" Mary murmured in wonder. "No smoke stains!" While the children waited in the car, the astonished adults walked around, avoiding the still-smoking bales of hay, inspecting everything carefully. The propane tank stood in its usual place, the pickup was undamaged, and the barn was the same as always. How could this be? All of it had been right in the way of the hungry flames.

Judy looked down at the charred earth, and sudden shivers ran through her. "Joe, look!" There lay the answer to everything. She and her husband were standing inside a large circle of green grass, which stretched all around their buildings, the tank, and the pickup. Everything outside the ring had been ruined. But inside the circle was a safe haven, a hug in the midst of chaos. Soon Judy would also learn that the cows, in the path of the blaze too, had been rounded up and moved to a safe corner of the pasture. Yet none of the firefighters had done it.

God, give us a wall of angels. Judy remembered the unbelievable plea that the prayer chain had sent heavenward. Was anything impossible with God? Joy filled her as she went to bring her children home.

THE LIGHT OF LOVE

We shall find peace. We shall hear the angels,
we shall see the sky sparkling with diamonds.

—ANTON PAVLOVICH CHEKHOV

It was Thanksgiving weekend, and Andrew Koval, an avid sports-man, decided to take advantage of the weather. "I'm going hunt-ing," he called to his wife. "I'll be back at five-thirty." Andrew knew his limits; due to an old baseball injury, one of his knees was good for about two hours of walking before pain set in. In addition, dark-ness would fall at about five o'clock, and since it was already late in the day, his time was short.

Andrew drove to his favorite hunting spot a few miles from his home in rural Cambridge, Ohio, just down the road from a farm where he bought hay every spring. He parked in a familiar hilly area near a field.

He walked awhile, flushed a few grouse out of their hiding places, but never got close enough to try a shot. And, as he slowly realized, his heart wasn't really in the sport today. "My nephew John Grimes had died of cancer the past summer," Andrew explains. "We had been very close, working and golfing and socializing together, but most of all, hunting grouse together." Andrew had grieved deeply for the younger man, and now, in this place where they'd spent so much time together, doubts crowded his mind. Was there really a God? If so, did Andrew believe in him? Was there a heaven? Was John there? Did life, another kind of life, go on after death? As a self-described lukewarm Catholic, Andrew "still had that little doubt." How could he know for sure?

Andrew had been lost in thought for some time, but it was getting dark, and his expedition was over for the day. He started back to the car. "On the way, I flushed a grouse and decided to follow it to get off at least one shot. The bird flew in the opposite direction, but being in familiar territory, I wasn't concerned." As the sun began to set, Andrew lost sight of the bird.

No problem, he told himself. The terrain was wooded, but he knew about where he was. If he walked back in a straight line, he ought to reach the car in about fifteen minutes. And that's what he did, or thought he did. But soon Andrew realized he had passed the same marker twice. He was going in a circle.

What to do? "I was wearing a light hunting vest, and it was getting colder," he says. "My knee had started to hurt. I kept walking west, trying to reach an area that I recognized." Surely he would hit a road soon and be able to flag down a vehicle. He walked and walked, only to realize that he was again traveling in a circle. He thought again of his resourceful young nephew, who would surely have found the way out of this maze.

Cold and tired, his knee throbbing, Andrew knew his wife and son were going to be very worried. How long would it be before they alerted the sheriff? If only he had a cell phone. Should he try to build a temporary shelter and wait to be found? Could he withstand a winter night with a vest as his only warmth?

There was another option, although he didn't think of it right away. He could pray. It had been a long time since Andrew had really talked to God. But if God were everywhere, even here in this lonely forest, he would surely hear. Andrew sat down under a tree. "God," he whispered. "I don't know if you're listening. But if you are, I need help."

More minutes passed, and a plan came to him. He should climb the highest hill, look for a light, and head straight for it. It was almost as if God were whispering in his ear, "Look for the light." Andrew didn't know if it was God's voice or not. But there was a high hill nearby.

Gathering the last of his failing strength, Andrew staggered to the top. At last! He ought to be able to see a lot of the countryside from here. But he could hardly believe it. There was no light visible, not in any direction. No distant signal blinking from a house or store, not even car headlights moving in the blackness.

It hadn't been a heavenly message, after all. Yet the feeling of comfort and guidance had been so real. *Look for the light.* Andrew understood just then that the real light in his life ought to be God, no matter what happened to him now or in the future. His leg ached, and his fear of freezing was strong. But he had felt the light, just a little, and he wouldn't let it dim again.

Slowly, he turned away. He would go back down the hill and wait. Andrew gazed into the blackness once more, his eyes narrowing. Was it a mirage? No, there in the distance . . . It *was* a light! Not in the same direction as his car, but Andrew had run out of choices. He would go toward it. Whoever owned it might have a phone, or warmth, or some way to help him.

"I must have walked at least another mile, but I was able to keep the light in view the whole time, despite the trees," Andrew says. Unexpectedly, he came upon the road where he had parked his car. It was sitting right there!

Astonished, Andrew scrambled inside, turning on the engine and the heater full blast. Soon he was blissfully warm and content, as if this terrible experience had never happened. He should get home now, to relieve his wife's fears.

But oddly, he could still see the light streaming from a field about three or four hundred yards down the road, near the farm he visited each spring. He was so late already—it wouldn't make much difference if he drove down and looked to see exactly what had brought him safely out of his ordeal. So he decided to go take a look.

"There in the field was a two-story house, every room brightly lit, with two floodlights on each corner," he says. "There were people working all around, both inside and out." Andrew remembered then that this land was owned by a real estate agent and was for sale in five-acre lots. He had no idea that a house had already been built here. "I thought it was strange that I hadn't known, and also that every room was blazing with light and there was so much activity." But he had his answer, and he turned around in the house's driveway and went home.

It was almost nine o'clock by the time Andrew arrived, and his worried wife was preparing to call the sheriff and arrange a search party. But he assured her he was none the worse for wear, and told her about the house. "I haven't heard about any construction over there," his wife mused. "But wasn't it fortunate that you saw the lights?"

Andrew didn't grouse hunt for the rest of the season. But when spring arrived, he decided it was time to visit the local farmer and buy his straw. Andrew turned onto the same county road where he had seen the house, and he began to look for it. Now he would see if it was as big and beautiful—and busy—during the day as it had looked on that memorable night. Maybe he would even pull into the driveway, ring the doorbell, and tell the owner how his marvelous lights had probably saved Andrew's life.

Andrew approached the lot where the house had been. But there was no building there, or anywhere around it. The area looked just as it had last spring when Andrew had come to buy his straw. Completely deserted.

He was certainly looking at the same spot where he had been that night—he remembered the familiar markers, the hills beyond, and the driveway where he'd turned around. Had the people who built the house belatedly discovered that their well was inadequate? This had happened before, and when it did, an owner would occasionally have his house moved to another lot.

Andrew went past the lot and pulled into the farm driveway. The farmer's sister came out to greet him. After purchasing his straw, Andrew paused for a moment. "I was wondering what happened to that big new house down the road," he asked.

The woman looked puzzled. "What house?"

"The one with all the lights. In the new subdivision. Did they have to move it because of a bad well?"

"I don't know what you're talking about. The builder never sold any of those lots. There has never been a house there."

"But . . ." Andrew felt a shiver. The woman was looking at him as if he were a bit odd. He didn't say any more, but he knew what he had seen.

Andrew has never found any evidence that a house was on that lot, or anywhere around there. But he is as sure today as he was that night that it was there. "I have come to believe that God was responsible for it," he says, "because the whole experience completely resolved any doubts I may have had about him, and about the continuance of life after death on earth." And perhaps his nephew was involved, too. One never knows, when one is willing to ask, just what marvels the Light will bring.

A MOTHER'S JOB

A mother's love for her child is like nothing else in the world.
It knows no law, no pity, it dares all things and crushes down
remorselessly all that stands in its path.

—AGATHA CHRISTIE

Several years ago Suzan King* read a book written by Catherine Marshall, author of the beloved titles *Christy* and *A Man Called Peter.* Catherine was a great believer in intercessory prayer. At that time, Suzan was a self-described "brand-new Christian. I had been born and raised Lutheran—and if you'd asked me, I would have said I was a Christian. But I didn't have a personal relationship with Jesus."

Recently, however, Suzan's life had become difficult. Her four daughters were teenagers, and there was turbulence in their home; one girl had moved out and another had run away. Suzan had medical problems, too. One day, realizing that she was at the end of

*All names in this story have been changed.

her rope, she had knelt in desperation. "Lord," she prayed, "Come and take my life into your hands." And he had done so.

Now Suzan was reading books and looking for people to help her develop in this new and deeper relationship with God. "Gradually, he brought godly women into my life, and when they saw my desire to get closer to him, they began to train me in my faith and practice." One in particular taught her more about intercessory prayer. Suzan felt that God was calling her to pray in this way more intentionally and regularly.

She began during her morning walks. There was something about the autumn air, the scents and sights of nature, that allowed her to feel close to God. She prayed primarily for the daughter who had run away, asking that God keep her safe and bring her back. But soon, another family problem loomed. One morning, her second-oldest, Charlotte, told Suzan that Beth, the youngest, was planning a secret date that evening with a boy she knew her mom and dad would not like.

"Tom and I had always insisted that we meet and approve any boy our daughters dated," Suzan explains. "Beth was obviously breaking that rule."

After breakfast, Suzan immediately went for her walk. "God," she prayed, "if Tom and I confront Beth about this, she might defy us or, worse, move out. I don't think I could survive that again, with another daughter. But if we don't say anything, she'll get away with it. How should I pray for her? What shall I ask?"

Suzan waited a moment. Was it her imagination, or did she hear specific words moving in her heart? "Pray for intervention," was the message.

Intervention. Didn't that mean asking God to take control of the *whole* situation? This was chancy. But Suzan was in a foxhole, with no other answers in sight. And she knew God respected her free will enough to refrain from acting until she asked him to do so. "God, please intervene," she prayed. "Work your will in this situation."

Immediately she was flooded with peace. She had done what God requested, and the rest was up to him.

As evening approached, Suzan behaved as if nothing were amiss. She wondered how God would resolve the situation, or if it would be resolved. Perhaps she would have to stand by and watch Beth actually leave, pretending that she did not know about the secret date. Could she do it? She had thought she might be tempted to take the problem back from God and to confront Beth after all. But oddly, she remained calm. "It was," she says, "as if the Holy Spirit had given me a supernatural gift of faith."

A few hours before the date, Beth came home unexpectedly from her after-school job. "I've got a terrible toothache," she told her mother. "I made a dentist appointment for tomorrow, but I'm going to bed now." Suzan was amazed. Beth had never had a toothache before (nor has she had one since). But the secret date had obviously been canceled.

The following Friday, however, Charlotte told Suzan that the date was on again for Saturday right after work. "God," Suzan asked, "what should I do this time?"

Again the unmistakable answer came. "Pray for intervention." Suzan did. She was almost not surprised when Beth got ready to leave for work on Saturday morning and discovered that her car battery was dead. "I guess Dad will have to drive you and pick you up from work today," Suzan told her daughter. Beth nodded glumly. Another plan foiled!

Beth made another secret plan and another. In every case, her mother prayed for intervention. In every case, the plan failed. Eventually, since they were never able to go out together, Beth lost interest in the boy. "The most amazing part about it all was that none of the circumstances obstructing Beth's plans had any direct connection with her dad or me," Suzan says. "So we were able to keep our already fragile relationship intact."

Through the next several years, the bond between Tom and Suzan and their daughters grew deeper, more peaceful. One morning during her senior year in college, however, Beth phoned. "I'm not coming home for the Christmas holidays, Mom."

"But why?" Suzan was shocked. Their oldest daughter was bringing her new baby home for Christmas, and the family was looking forward to being together.

"I'm going to South Dakota to spend Christmas with my roommate's family." Beth explained.

"Well, if that's what you really want . . ." Suzan stayed calm. But as soon as she hung up she began the familiar pattern of prayer. "God, please intervene," she asked. "Work out your will for Beth over the holidays. If you want her to go to South Dakota, I won't get in your way."

Suzan sensed immediately that God did not want Beth to go to South Dakota. In fact, Suzan was certain that Beth had a "divine appointment" already scheduled at home.

Of course, she said nothing to Beth when they spoke the following week. "I'm working out the plans for South Dakota," Beth explained confidently. "And if I can't get a flight, I just met a boy who's driving there, and he says I can ride along."

A boy she barely knew . . . And what if the weather turned dangerous? Suzan remained noncommittal. But after the call, she stormed heaven again—just in case God had been occupied elsewhere!

The following week, Beth called again. "Mom, I can't believe it! I couldn't get a ticket on any flight—they're all booked. And that driver canceled, too. No matter what arrangements I try to make, they all fall through!" Beth paused, and Suzan had the feeling that her daughter was getting suspicious. "Mom, do you know anything about this?"

Suzan smiled. The girls were catching on to her heavenly pipe-line. "Honey, I just think you're supposed to be here."

"Well, I'm giving up. I'll be home for Christmas."

It was the best gift Suzan would receive. But there was more in store. That week, a Christian organization in the area arranged a party for the college sons and daughters of those who worked with them. And when Beth attended, she met a young man named John. John's parents were missionaries, and the entire family had just returned from an assignment on the other side of the world. Interestingly, Beth's dad knew John's dad, and the two had once talked about how compatible their children might be!

"John had grown up overseas, thousands of miles from where we lived," Suzan says. "But God arranged for him to come to our town at just the right time to meet Beth, a girl he never would have met had she gone to South Dakota that Christmas."

The families were delighted but not really surprised when John and Beth married. Nor has Suzan been surprised to learn that the couple prays over their little son, Philip, all the time. They ask God to intervene, to let Philip know Jesus at an early age, and to find their son a godly woman when the time is right. And why not? John and Beth have learned from an "expert" that life works best when we let God take charge.

THE HOMECOMING

Seems that God is looking more for ways to get us home than for ways to keep us out. I challenge you to find one soul who came to God seeking grace and did not find it.

—MAX LUCADO, *WHEN GOD WHISPERS YOUR NAME*

As Suzan and other parents know, troubles with children are probably the most painful times of life. Mike and Susan Rheaume are a compatible, spiritual couple whose lives revolved around their two sons, Mike Jr. and Andy. Although Andy was somewhat of a loner, he was also an obedient son and an affectionate brother. That was why it was such a shock to Mike and Susan when Andy turned eighteen and abruptly announced he was moving out of the house. "I just don't want to live here anymore," he told his parents. "I'll finish high school, but I want to be on my own."

"Why?" Susan asked, stunned.

Andy shrugged. He couldn't offer any answers, at least none that his parents could comprehend.

During his final semester, Andy stayed with friends or lived on the streets. He attended classes and wrestling practice every day, and caused no problems. In the absence of delinquency, drug use, or truancy, school officials told Mike and Susan that they couldn't intervene. Andy was a legal adult. There was no way his parents could force him to live in their house.

After graduation, Andy seemingly had a change of heart. He moved back home and prepared to attend a Christian college on a wrestling scholarship. But after a semester, he lost interest in school. He returned home briefly, then left again—for a life on the streets.

Mike and Susan were heartbroken. Their son was now part of the homeless population! It was hard to bear the thought of him, cold and hungry, choosing to live in a cardboard box or other appalling surroundings. "I would go out looking for him, to try and persuade him to come home, or to bring blankets and food," Mike says. "Sometimes he lived in a rusted-out car near a junkyard—I'd leave things there for him." But despite their efforts, Andy grew more and more distant. Eventually he took a job selling magazine subscriptions and left the area.

Several months later, Mike and Susan got a call from Andy. He was in South Dakota with his girlfriend, who was expecting a child. Could they come home?

Mike and Susan longed to rescue their son, although they were hesitant about these new circumstances. They drove to South

Dakota, collected Andy and his girlfriend, and explained on the way back that the young couple could live with them until the baby was born, if certain conditions were met. "We wanted Andy to join the mainstream, to get a job and straighten up," Mike says. "We told them we wouldn't give them access to our credit cards, or money to spend. They would have to treat us fairly and take responsibility for themselves." Andy and his girlfriend initially agreed to the terms.

But shortly before Thanksgiving, Mike discovered that some of his money was missing. At the same time, Susan realized that the young couple had been using her credit cards. When she confronted them, reminding them of their agreement, an argument ensued. Andy and his girlfriend stormed out of the house.

"We assumed they would cool off and come back," Susan says. "But months passed, and we had no word from them. Still, they were in the area—people would see them and call us. And when the baby was born at a nearby hospital, we sent flowers with a note: 'We love you and want you in our lives.'" But Andy and his family did not respond. Eventually, they dropped completely from sight. Mike asked a friend knowledgeable in finding people to track the couple, but after three months he reported failure. "Your son is either living far underground, maybe on the streets," the investigator reported, "or he's dead."

Susan and Mike had always had a network of supportive relatives and friends, mainly from their church community, St. Thomas of Villanova, in Palatine, Illinois. Now, that group reached out to the couple. As months passed with no word from Andy, people began to pray for him. Others attended morning Mass on his behalf. Encouraging notes appeared in the Rheaumes' mailbox. At one point, during the second year of Andy's absence, a group held a prayer service for him, asking God to protect him and his family and bring them safely home.

Such support was critical to Mike and Susan for, by now, their grief was profound. "When something like this happens, it's almost like going through a death, except that nothing ends," Susan says. "You worry and imagine the worst. Is our son ill, or dead? What about our grandchild—will we ever find him or her? You relive events from the past, asking yourself: What did we do wrong? Could we have prevented any of this?"

Mike wondered angrily why God was permitting this to happen to them. Hadn't they always done their best for their children and for God? Hadn't they prayed together faithfully, read and taught Scripture, made God the center of their lives? Such questions were natural, given their situation. But as months wore on, Mike came to the only conclusion he could: God was in charge, and God would see it all through.

As Christmas 1994 approached, Mike began to believe that one more step was needed. Their close friends and family knew about

Andy's absence, but perhaps more people should be praying. Andy's birthday was December 29. What if they asked not only their close friends but also their long-distance relatives, friends from long ago, even business acquaintances, everyone on their Christmas card list—all 124—to pray for Andy on his birthday?

This was risky; in a world where everyone should "have it all together," it's difficult to expose your wounds, especially when they involve family problems. Would people become uncomfortable around Mike and Susan, even turn away from them? Would they be judged instead of consoled?

And yet, there is great power in prayer. If it could not banish Mike and Susan's sorrow or bring them answers, perhaps it would provide the courage they needed to continue their lonely walk. After much thought, Mike inserted a little note in each Christmas card: "Please pray for Andy on December 29," and dropped everything in the mail.

"The minute people received the cards, our phone began to ring," Susan recalls. "From everywhere, the universal response was: 'Why should we wait until Andy's birthday? We just wanted you to know we're praying *now*.'" It was a complete outpouring of love and acceptance, and as Christmas drew nearer, Susan and Mike felt sustained, even carried. Others, all across the country, every moment, were helping them bear this awful burden.

On the evening of December 23, as Susan's large extended family noisily arrived to begin the holidays, the phone rang. Mike answered it.

"Dad?" The voice on the other end was different, yet very familiar.

"Andy? Is it you?" Mike could hardly believe his ears. The hubbub in the room suddenly stopped.

"Yeah." There was a silence. "I live in California now."

Someone was running for Susan, telling her to pick up the extension. She did, but she couldn't talk. She could only weep.

Andy's relationship had crumbled, and he had sole custody of his daughter, Moriah, a three year old who had cerebral palsy. He had also fathered two other children, in two other relationships, both of which had ended. Mike and Susan were somewhat stunned. This was not the news they had hoped to hear. Yet Andy was alive, and they had grandchildren too. During those lonely, agonizing nights of prayer, had they ever asked for more than this?

Mike made a quick decision. "Do you want to come home for Christmas, Andy?" he asked.

Susan, on the other phone, held her breath. "Yes," she heard her son say slowly. "I do."

Mike assured him that they would arrange for plane tickets and pick up Andy and Moriah at the airport in twenty-four hours, on Christmas Eve. Before he hung up, Mike had a final question. "Andy, it's been almost four years since we've talked to you. Why did you call now?"

Another silence. "I don't know."

Today, Mike and Susan discuss their son and his life with evident relief, for he has moved back from California. But there is still sorrow mixed with the gladness, for Andy's life continues to be somewhat erratic. But Moriah brings a special, unexpected joy. And the story hasn't ended yet.

"One of our friends, considering Andy's situation, laughed and said, 'Perhaps we should have prayed more specifically,'" Susan says. "But I believe that this is God's miracle. He started it, and he's going to finish it. Our job is to love and to pray and to wait upon him."

They won't be waiting alone. Andy may not know why he had that sudden impulse to phone his parents, but they do. They and the 124 families who gave the most important gift of all—faith.

PART 2

HELP FROM THE ANGELS

ALLIE'S ANGEL

I saw them with my bodily eyes as clearly as I see you. And when they departed, I used to weep and wish they would take me with them.

—St. Joan of Arc

When Mother's Day rolls around, Lynn Levitin of West Bloomfield, Michigan, enjoys every minute of it, for her path to maternity has been more anxious than most. She remembers all too clearly the irrational fear she began to exhibit almost at the start of her second pregnancy; she felt certain that something was very wrong. "My doctor tried to reassure me that the baby and I were both fine, but there was nothing he could say or do that would put my mind at rest," she says. There seemed to be no reason for her concern, so there was no logical way to combat it. Eventually, Lynn went through a normal delivery and gave birth to a healthy baby girl, and she hoped her strange fears had gone. But when little Alexandra was just ten days old, Lynn suddenly "knew" what her unease was all about. "As I was feeding her one night, I looked at our reflection in the mirror. There seemed to be a covering over her, like a gauzy white sheet. I took that vision as a warning—that although she appeared perfectly healthy, she needed medical attention immediately." Lynn woke her husband, and he reluctantly took them to the hospital emergency room.

"The ER staff were extremely kind and thorough, and they ran all kinds of tests, though they had nothing to go on because the baby appeared perfectly healthy. They finally sent me home with the reassurance that all was normal." But Lynn's overwhelming feelings of dread and unrest continued. "Several days later, after talking to her pediatrician for the hundredth time, I took her to the ER of yet another hospital." The same tests were administered, with the same results. Little Allie was as healthy as any baby could be.

This time, however, Lynn refused to sign the discharge papers. "The baby is going to be ill very soon, and she needs to be here when it happens!" she insisted.

One of the physicians slipped out to call for a psychiatrist. "Probably a postpartum-induced psychosis," murmured another. But in the interim, they sent yet another doctor to see Allie. After thoroughly examining her, he looked at Lynn. "I need you to tell me what is wrong with your daughter," he said gently.

At last! Someone who seemed to take her seriously! But what could she tell him? Lynn looked at the baby, and the baby looked right back. Their eyes locked for a moment, and suddenly Lynn knew. "You need to focus on her abdomen," she said. "That's where the problem is."

"Very well." The doctor nodded. "We'll do a CT scan tomorrow morning."

"No! You have to do it now!" Lynn was adamant.

"It's very late in the day—"

"Now!" Tears pricked her eyes. "I don't think she'll make it through the night."

Oddly, the doctor complied. Just a short time later, the results showed that Allie was filled with fluid and had peritonitis. Within an hour, she was in surgery, where physicians removed a portion of her colon. But they could not find the source of the peritonitis. "The doctor came out to talk to us, and he gently warned us that she might not live through the night," Lynn says. "He explained that it was difficult enough operating on a healthy newborn, but Allie was so sick that her resistance was much lower. Yet somehow I knew she would be fine." Following a very lengthy hospital stay and recuperation period, baby Allie was discharged.

"Watch over her closely for the first five years," the doctors advised. Because they hadn't found the cause of her illness, they could not be sure it wouldn't return. However, to this day it remains a mystery.

Alexandra developed well, and as she approached her second birthday, she started to talk. But her first word was not *mama* or *dada*. It was *angel*. As her verbal skills developed, she told her family that her angel's name was Bummer, that he was a very tall man, at least eight feet, and seemed a playful person. "Frankly, I chalked it up to an imaginary friend," Lynn says, "until odd things started happening in the house. For example, one day I was looking for a book for my son. I turned the house upside down, but since Allie was only three, I didn't include her in this search." While Lynn was still looking, the toddler approached, carrying the book.

"Here, Mommy," she said, holding it out. "Bummer said you wanted this. He told me where it was."

On several other occasions, Lynn would be in an adjacent room and hear Allie happily chattering away at Bummer. "One day I heard a deep male voice talking back to her," Lynn says. "I ran into the next room, but she was alone. I thought I was hearing things, until the day my husband came to me and said he heard our daughter talking to someone, and a male voice responding." And late one night Lynn was reading in her family room when she heard two sets of footsteps running across Allie's hardwood floors just over her head, and the unmistakable sound of Allie's giggling. "I couldn't believe my two kids had gotten up and were playing so late," Lynn says. But as she reached the upstairs landing she saw her son in his bedroom, fast asleep. Allie, however, was just jumping into her bed, still laughing. "Allie, what are you up to?" Lynn asked.

"Bummer and I were playing, Mommy," Allie reported, "but he told me it was time to go to bed now."

There *had* been two sets of footsteps, Lynn knew for sure. "We learned to leave her alone during these times, and we respected her visits with Bummer."

Time passed, and one day the family was vacationing in Florida. Allie awakened suddenly, in tears. "Honey, what's the matter?" Lynn asked in alarm.

"It's Bummer," Allie sobbed. "He says it's time for him to go. He'll always be close by, but . . ."

"Where did Bummer say he was going?" Lynn asked.

Allie pointed to the sky.

Had it been a dream? No, the little girl was inconsolable, too upset to be comforted. Lynn could only try to distract her. "Don't be sad, honey," she said. "Remember, you're turning five tomorrow, and we're going to have a wonderful party for you with cake and presents—" And then Lynn remembered.

The doctors had told her that her daughter would need to be "watched" for the first five years of her life. And so Allie had been watched, more closely and tenderly than any of them had ever suspected.

Bummer reappeared a few times during that next year, perhaps to ease Allie's sadness over their separation, and he seems to be quite near the family even now, for Lynn has learned to sense a certain presence. As is typical with children who have these mystical experiences, Allie, now fifteen, remembers Bummer as if in a dream rather than as an actual being. But Lynn knows that he was real. "Many angels probably helped me through that difficult time," she says. "I know they understand how grateful I am."

WHEN MOM AND THE ANGELS JOIN FORCES

I don't see how I possibly could have come from where I entered the planet to where I am now if there had not been angels along the way.

—DELLA REESE

D aryl Messenger of Byron, Illinois, will admit that her son's mere existence is proof that angels take care of us. For there are some children who just naturally seem to gravitate toward trouble— and Gary Treese has always been one of them. He was already walking, actually running, by the time he was eight months old, and the activity never ceased. "When he was eighteen months old, he fell on an aluminum folding chair and sliced his little face from cheek to cheek across his nose," Daryl remembers. "That was the first of many trips to the emergency room." When Gary was about six, he fell off his minibike wearing only a pair of summer shorts, slid down a gravel road on his tummy, and narrowly missed impaling himself on a steel spike on the side of the road. (The neighbors, used to this, picked him up and sent him home.) On two separate occasions while deer hunting, Gary climbed into his tree stand and promptly dozed off. He fell to the ground each time, breaking his shoulder. Given his love for demolition-derby cars (which he built with his dad), and his hunting and snowmobiling mishaps, Gary was a regular at the doctor's office.

Daryl had been divorced when Gary was a baby, and a few years later, she married the man Gary always regarded as his father. Both adults were bewildered over their son's constant mishaps. Daryl never knew what kind of catastrophe—stitches? a cast?—would greet her when she returned home from work. It certainly made life interesting, but Daryl sometimes felt guilty. Shouldn't she be able to prevent some of these episodes?

Amazingly, Gary survived his high-school years (despite two motorcycle accidents). Through her constant prayers for her son's safety and health, Daryl grew closer to Jesus, and eventually became a Christian. During this time, she learned about angels. She knew they were supposed to guard us. Could she possibly put them in charge of Gary? By now, her son was an adult, but she still worried about his safety. "One day, I told Jesus that I was giving my son to him to care for because I could no longer watch and worry when the next accident would hit." She also asked Jesus to surround her son with angels.

One winter night a few months later, Gary went out with some of his buddies. It was 1:30 a.m. when he set out for home on his snowmobile. Gary rode this route often, even in the dark, and although he had to cross a river to get home, he wasn't at all concerned. Eventually, he saw the river ahead, set into gently rolling hills and no doubt still frozen over. There was a bike path along the bridge that Gary could have taken to cross the river, but as always, he preferred a challenge. Revving his engine, he flew down the side of the hill, hoping to gain enough speed to cross the ice to a flat riverbank on the opposite side. But his strategy failed, for as he shot across the river, he realized that the spring thaw had already begun. To his horror, as he reached the middle of the river, the ice gave way. He and his snowmobile started to sink.

Tearing off his gloves and helmet, Gary struggled to swim. But it seemed impossible. His heavy clothing was pulling him under the jagged ice. His snowmobile disappeared. The water was so terribly cold, and the riverbank seemed miles away. He realized that he would die here. His mother would be heartbroken.

Panicked, he again attempted to swim, but it was hard to see anything now that the snowmobile headlight had sunk. *Swim, swim,* he told himself. *You have to get out of here.* Was that the bank right in front of him? Yes. But how had he gotten across? He was soaked all the way through, but still, somehow, afloat.

Gary grabbed for the bank. But it was covered with ice, and his frozen hands kept slipping. When he did get a grip, the ice would break and he would lose ground. Kicking, he tried to get closer, but he was exhausted and falling asleep now. Sinking into the bitterly cold water, sinking . . .

Suddenly, Gary awakened. He was standing up, out of the water. He looked around in disbelief. Had the accident been a dream? No, he was soaking wet, his teeth chattering, and standing on a snow-covered hill that led up to the highway. How had this happened? He was completely alone, so who could have pulled him out? Yet there was the highway, and headlights were approaching. Gary staggered to the side of the road, waving his arms. Seeing him, the driver pulled over. "Son," he leaned out of the window. "Do you need help?"

At about 2:30 a.m., Daryl's husband answered the phone. A friend of Gary's wanted them to come to his house right away. Gary had had a snowmobile accident, but a kind truck driver had delivered him there. Daryl was adamant that the paramedics be called, and Gary's friends did that. "At first, the doctors thought he might lose his fingers and toes due to frostbite," Daryl says. "But he didn't, and is now fully recovered."

The following morning, Daryl drove past the spot where her son almost drowned. One of Gary's gloves was lying out on the river, embedded in the ice. There was no sign of the snowmobile. And in the snow, Daryl clearly saw *two* distinct sets of footprints leading from the river to the highway. "I knew then that angels had lifted my son from the icy waters up onto that bank. And I know that the Lord walked beside him and led him to help."

Recently, Gary damaged both his ankles in a fall, so Daryl admits that she cannot totally give up worrying about her son, especially one as active as he is. "But when I find myself involved in these little nagging thoughts, I stop myself and say, 'Lord, he is yours!' Then a sense of peace comes over me, and I know that, no matter what, Gary is safe in the Lord's hands." She knows miracles happen every day.

HOME ON A WING
AND A PRAYER

Preach always. When necessary, use words.

—ST. FRANCIS OF ASSISI

Virgil Gibson, of Meeker, Oklahoma, was a special man. Everyone who knew him recognized his kindness, generosity, and spiritual strength. "If anyone needed anything, they would call us," according to Kathleen Gibson. "They knew Virgil would help."

Kathleen was his biggest fan. "I always believed that God had brought us together, because we married after knowing each other just two weeks, and Virgil loved me unconditionally for thirty-one years." Every day was like a greeting card, and she could hardly wait to open it.

Virgil was a truck driver, who had named his company, A Wing and a Prayer. Kathleen rode with him as often as she could, and nearly always after their son grew up. "We were a team not only in trucking, but in life. Where you saw him, you would see me."

In 2001, Virgil developed some health problems, but he didn't want to retire. Kathleen could drive, they decided, and he would go along. "I would rather be with you in the truck than anywhere else," Virgil told Kathleen, "especially if anything ever happened to me." Kathleen didn't want to think about that.

During the winter of 2002, the couple drove a load from Chicago to Jacksonville, Florida, and had to stay there over the weekend before picking up another load for the return journey. This was not unusual. Kathleen and Virgil passed the time in their truck, watching television and enjoying each other's company as usual.

On Monday morning, as they left the truck-stop restaurant, Virgil stopped abruptly. "I'm dizzy," he told Kathleen. Then he fell to the ground.

"Virgil!" Quickly, Kathleen reached into his pocket for his nitroglycerine pills.

People ran toward them. One trucker called an ambulance, while others surrounded the pair. Kathleen knelt on the pavement with Virgil's head in her lap. The scene seemed surreal. How could this be happening? She couldn't lose Virgil, God, she just couldn't! Looking up, she noticed an older couple approaching. The woman was carrying a Bible, and the man held blankets, which he tucked around Virgil's still form. Quietly, the woman began to pray.

The paramedics arrived, and as they applied electrodes to shock Virgil's heart, the woman drew Kathleen away from the scene. "Your husband is with God now," she said quietly. "God is going to put his arms around you and help you through this grief."

No, it wasn't true! But somehow Kathleen knew the woman was right. As Virgil was put into the ambulance, the woman led Kathleen back to it and helped her in. During the long ride to Ed Fraser Memorial Hospital in Macclenny, Florida, Kathleen continued to pray: "Please God, save my husband. I love him. I need him."

The doctors did all that they could, but the lady at the truck stop had been right. Virgil had already entered paradise.

Kathleen was exhausted when she finally walked out of the emergency room. There was so much to do, so much sorrow to bear, and she was alone in an unfamiliar city. How was she going to cope? But when she approached the waiting room, she stopped in surprise. Sitting peacefully in the room was the couple from the truck stop! "We're supposed to be here," the man explained, brushing aside Kathleen's astonished thanks. "We knew you'd need a ride back."

She looked at them closely for the first time. Two ordinary, gray-haired grandparent–types, perhaps in their late sixties. She had never seen them before—and she knew many truckers. But despite the shock and grief that were just beginning to move through her, she felt comfortable, safe, even somehow loved. The lady was still holding her Bible. "Come," she told Kathleen. "You need to eat.

You have to keep up your strength." Borne along by their energy, Kathleen could do nothing but obey.

Her newfound friends barely left her side for the rest of the day. They took Kathleen to a local mortuary to make the final arrangements. With their help, Kathleen contacted her sister, who instructed her to stay in Jacksonville until family members could come to her the next day. The couple also moved their truck right next to Kathleen's. She noticed that they weren't pulling a trailer. "We don't need one right now," the man explained.

That seemed strange. "Have you been driving long?" Kathleen persisted.

The woman smiled. "Not long at all," she answered comfortably.

None of it made sense. Surely they were supposed to be driving a load somewhere. But when Kathleen realized that they were going to stay all night right alongside her, she broke down. "I'm so sorry for being such a burden," she began. The couple wouldn't listen.

"This is what people are supposed to do for each other," the man stated firmly.

"We're just getting you over this hump," his wife pointed out. "But as long as you keep God number one in your life, you're going to be just fine." Kathleen knew that. Once again, despite her sorrow, she sensed an unexpected peace.

When Kathleen awakened the following morning, the couple and their truck were gone. "I asked the waitress if they had come in to eat breakfast," Kathleen says, "but she hadn't seen them since the night before when they were with me." Perhaps they simply hadn't wanted to awaken Kathleen. She would miss them. Without their kindness and steady reassurance, she wondered how she would have managed.

It wasn't until Kathleen was back in Meeker that she began to wonder more specifically about the pair. Where had they come from? How had they seemed to know so much? Most important, had she adequately expressed her gratitude to them? She hadn't even asked their names.

Fortunately, she remembered the company logo on the truck they were driving. She would contact their employer, tell him how lucky he was to have workers who were so good, so caring of others. But when she phoned Information, she learned that there was no such listing for the company anywhere in the country. Nor, through any of her industry contacts, was she ever able to locate the company or the drivers.

Kathleen died recently, and we who knew her are sure that Virgil came to meet her—along with two special angels to guide her home.

ANGELS OF WARMTH
AND COMFORT

The footprints of an angel are love. And where there is love,
miraculous things can happen.
—*ANGELS IN THE OUTFIELD*

Twelve-year-old Nancy Petti (now Doran) and her family had recently come to the Bronx in New York from their native Italy. Their decision to do so was born out of great hope, for many times Nancy's father had attempted to start his own business in Italy and at one point had even left the family temporarily to try the same thing in Germany. Eventually, her parents had decided that America offered the best chance of professional success for themselves and their children.

Nancy, her older brother, and younger sisters had been excited about the move, but apprehensive, too. What did America look like?

Was it similar to the movies they saw? Would they make new friends? Of course there would be challenges as they became accustomed to an unfamiliar language and new housing, jobs, and schools. But God had guided them through this formidable journey, and Nancy's parents firmly believed he would continue to take care of them.

Nancy wished she had the same faith as her mother and father. Yes, she was becoming accustomed to a lot of things in her new country. But no one had warned her about the cold weather. As that first winter tightened its grip on New York, Nancy could hardly believe how brutal the cold was, especially inside their apartment. "We didn't have much money, so this top-floor unit was all we could afford," she remembers. "But the landlord refused to give steam heat, and the temperature was so low you could see your breath. We usually wore coats and blankets during the day, and the oven was always on, with a pot of boiling water on the stove top for steam."

Even worse were the nights. Without a dense layer of blankets, "it felt as though the apartment had no walls and that we were actually sleeping outside."

Oh, why had they risked everything to come here? Nancy felt abandoned and lost. It was hard to be positive when your fingers and toes ached and you couldn't do your homework or even sleep because you shivered so much.

One bitter night, Nancy awakened and lay in the dark. She had curled into a little ball, trying to keep as warm as possible, but it wasn't working. She felt numb, as if she had turned to ice, and her thin blanket had slipped off her shoulders. Nancy tried to pull the blanket up to her chin. But her arms were stiff, and they wouldn't work! Was she freezing to death? "Oh, God, I'm so cold I can't even pick up my covers," she prayed. "Please help me."

Suddenly the room began to glow. It became brighter and brighter. What was happening? Nancy rubbed her eyes in wonder. There, right in front of her, stood a beautiful angel. Italy was filled with statues of angels—Nancy knew what these beings were. But *this* angel wasn't made of plaster. She was alive! "She had shimmering blonde hair, her eyes were a brilliant blue, and she wore a white flowing gown. Even more extraordinary was the light that radiated from within and all around her." What a beautiful creature! And she was visiting *Nancy,* in this cold, drab apartment! Nancy drank in the sight.

Tenderly, the angel smiled at her. Then she bent over, gently picked up Nancy's blanket, and pulled it up to the girl's chin. Nancy felt a burst of warmth, safety, and love. Instantly, the freezing room seemed filled with sunshine. Then the angel vanished.

Nancy didn't know it yet, but the risk her family took in coming to this new land would be rewarded. Not long after that night, her father was able to open a successful Italian restaurant. Nor did Nancy know that, despite future winters, she would never again be bothered by the cold.

But she knew one thing for certain: God was closer than she had ever imagined, and all she needed to do was simply reach out to him. His angels could find her wherever she was.

The cold rain had gone on since morning, keeping Bob Nance from his construction job and increasing his worry over finances. A lost day's pay was hard to make up. His family was getting very low on groceries. He paced back and forth in his little house, as his wife and mother-in-law fixed dinner in the kitchen and his three children played nearby. What if this deluge continued tomorrow?

"Dinner's ready!" Bob's wife called. Everyone headed for the table. Just then, Bob heard a knock on the front door. Who could be out in this storm?

He opened the door just a crack, to keep the cold air from coming in. On the porch stood a man about fifty years old, wearing a black suit, topcoat, and hat. Water ran down the hat's brim and dripped onto the man's already saturated coat. His shoes were sodden. "How can I help you?" Bob asked.

Despite his rumpled appearance, the stranger smiled. "The Lord said I should stop and talk with you."

Bob frowned. Was the man a crackpot? Surely he shouldn't invite him inside. And yet, there was something intriguing about him. Bob remembered the story of the innkeeper in Bethlehem so many centuries ago. He had always wondered if *he* could have found room for the holy family if the inn had been his. Well, he didn't have a hotel, but he did have a warm home. "Come in out of this weather, sir," he said, throwing open the door. "Let me take your wet things and dry them."

The visitor took off his hat, and Bob's oldest child, Dan, carried it to the kitchen to dry it beside the stove. Bob reached for the man's coat. "No, I'll just lay it over the back of this chair," the stranger said. The coat began to drip on the wooden floor. It looked as if it were soaked completely through.

The family made room for their unexpected visitor at the dinner table, and they shared their modest meal with him. Conversation flowed freely and pleasantly, "but we didn't talk of anything specifically religious," Bob recalls, "nor did our guest tell us much about himself." Yet the little scene seemed right, somehow, as if everyone there was sharing in an unspoken benediction. Bob felt his worries gently lifted from his shoulders. He knew that things would get better. Just as the food had stretched tonight to include the stranger, the Lord would stretch Bob's meager resources and help him care for his family. He was certain of it.

As the meal ended, the visitor got up. "Thank you all for this wonderful dinner." He smiled. "I'll have to be moving on now."

Young Dan brought back the stranger's hat, still quite wet, and gave it to him. Bob picked up the coat lying over the chair, and held it as the man slipped it on. The two walked to the door together and shook hands, and the visitor departed into the drizzle. Bob closed the door.

The realization hit him then that the stranger's coat had been completely dry.

But it couldn't have dried in that short time—the floor under it was still slippery with puddles! Bob flung open the front door. Although he had a clear view of his entire street, and the stranger had had only seconds to walk away, no one was there.

Slowly, Bob closed the door. "I think we just fed an angel," he told his wife. And even the rain seemed bright.

DREAM FROM THE ANGELS

The value of consistent prayer is not that He will hear us,
but that we will hear Him.

—WILLIAM McGILL

Michael Ansted and his wife, Anne, both elementary school-teachers, had moved to a small country town by the sea in New Zealand, where they built a home for themselves and their six children (they have seven now). Prayer was a regular part of their life. "We shared twenty-eight acres with another family, so there was plenty of space," he says. "One evening our children decided to camp out under some pines about two hundred yards from the house." The adults accompanied them to the site and, after clearing the ground, they lit a small fire to roast potatoes. "We ate and sang a few songs," Michael recalls. "Then we doused the fire, making sure it was out. Fire is always a danger here because almost everything is built out of timber."

Michael was glad that his children enjoyed some innocent fun that evening, because the next morning they had to make a somber journey. A friend's six-year-old daughter had been sleeping in a tent with a candle for illumination. The flame had set the tent on fire, killing the child. The Ansted family did not know the child well, but they were more than willing to make the rough twenty-mile trip to attend the funeral. Perhaps in some small way, they could bring consolation to the family.

The following morning, everyone set out, their vehicle bouncing over rutted country roads. By the time they had gone three miles, however, Michael was beginning to feel odd. "I sensed a prodding to turn around and go home. At first I paid no attention to it—we had to be at the funeral!—but the urge became stronger, and eventually I just couldn't ignore it anymore." He told Anne what he was feeling.

"I think you should turn back," she told him.

"But it's bizarre—there's no reason," he argued.

"Maybe not, but perhaps it's better to be safe." As a mother of a large family, Anne had learned over the years that God works in mysterious ways.

Safe! They were safe *now*. But Michael turned the car around and started home. The children were perplexed and getting restless, and the extra five miles of backtracking would probably make them late for the funeral. Yet his heart was pounding with the effort to control the unreasonable urge. *Get home, get home.* Finally, they pulled into the driveway. Everything looked normal, but Michael realized it would take time to check it all. He would have to miss the funeral. He hugged everyone, turned the car keys over to Anne, and watched as they drove away again.

Then he carefully checked the house and the yard. Everything normal, everything fine. What was he looking for? The strange urge was gone now, and he felt ridiculous. He had made a mountain out of a molehill. But there was a positive side to it. The day was warm, and quiet enough for him to take a nap, which rarely happened.

Sometime later, Michael awakened with a start. He could hear crackling, a fire burning. The sound encircled him, and for a disoriented moment, he thought he was at the scene of the fire that had killed his friend's little girl. But no. He was here, lying on his bed. He leaped up and rushed outside, looking for the blaze. But he could find no source for the sound that had been so loud that it seemed to be on the pillow beside him. It must have been a dream after all. Michael went back to bed and was soon asleep.

Again he was awakened by the same sound of twigs burning. "Living on a peninsula covered in bush and pine, you act fast," he says. "I was out of the bedroom again as if my feet had wings." This time Michael was determined to search even the outskirts of the property until he had solved the mystery.

But again, there was no fire. As he was about to return to the house, he remembered the previous night's campsite. "Making my way along the ridge, I saw a wisp of smoke. I ran back and filled a bucket and returned to find a steady plume of smoke issuing from the ground where our fire had been." Looking more attentively, Michael now saw that the fire had been lit on a mixture of earth and pine needles. Slowly, it had penetrated that flammable layer and was now burning underground.

Michael realized that, with the family gone for the day, everything would have gone unnoticed until the heat generated had set a large area ablaze—an area dry and eager to burn. Given the limited firefighting resources, some thousand acres could have gone up in flames, including his new home. This was a silent fire, hidden, with no crackling wood and smoke to attract attention. And if the underground fire had taken a long time to surface, his whole family might have been back and in bed before it erupted, with little or no way for them to escape.

Michael ran back and forth, filling numerous buckets, until the area was saturated and finally secure. Then he sat down to rest and to think. He had set out on a journey of concern, but had been told to go back. He had heard the noise of fire where there was no flame. He had been given the tools to prevent a tragedy. Had it been his guardian angel who'd alerted him? Or the spirit of the little girl, already sending gifts from paradise? And why had one family's child been taken away, while his offspring were apparently protected?

"I believe that we all have decisions to make, and until we have completed them, we will not be called home," Michael says. And in the meantime, he gives thanks to the loving God who has arranged it all.

ANGELS AT THE MALL

Hush! my dear, lie still and slumber,
Holy angels guard thy bed!
Heavenly blessing without number
Gently falling on thy head.

—"A CRADLE HYMN," ISAAC WATTS

Gene and Jennie Kogovsek grew up one street apart in their Cleveland neighborhood. Both attended St. Mary of the Assumption Church and grade school, married other spouses, and raised their families in the same neighborhood. Eventually, each was widowed. One night, St. Mary's held a reunion. Gene spotted Jennie and went over to greet her. While at her table, he felt an inner nudge to ask Jennie out, and by the end of the evening, he had done so. The rest proceeded as everyone hoped it would, and on October 7, 1999, they married. Jennie was sixty-nine, and Gene was sixty-six. "When we asked the pastor of St. Mary's to perform our ceremony, he assumed we would have a small wedding," Gene recalls. "He nearly fell over when we explained that everyone in our families would be part of the ceremony, and that amounted to our eight children and, at that time, our sixteen grandchildren." (They now have twenty-three.) Not to mention at least two hundred guests.

A few months later, in February 2000, the couple drove to Fremont, Indiana, so Gene could attend a meeting. Afterward, they planned to go shopping at one of the malls there. But rain began to fall, and when Gene returned to their hotel room after the meeting, Jennie was not there. Assuming that she had gone shopping alone, Gene went to the parking lot to see if the car was still there, and it was. Where could Jennie be, especially in the rain? Concerned, Gene returned to the room and noticed the phone's message button flashing. A hospital in Angola, Indiana, had just called. Gene was to hurry there. Two women had found Jennie on a sidewalk of a mall near the hotel. The women had called paramedics, stayed with her, and used their own coats to shelter her from the rain. Jennie had apparently suffered a severe hemorrhagic stroke.

Gene was shattered. Where was God? Why had this happened to Jennie, especially so soon after their wedding? But he had always been a man of prayer. As he moved through the next few days, he began to see God's hand at work everywhere.

Gene had never been to Angola, but he somehow drove those nine miles directly to the hospital without making a wrong turn.

The emergency-room doctor told him that, when questioned, Jennie could not remember much, so hospital personnel had looked in her purse. All of her identification was still in her former name, but Jennie also happened to be carrying a church bulletin from St. Mary's in Cleveland, the church where they had been married. Someone from the emergency room had called the church rectory.

"The call was made after noon," Gene says, "and the church secretary is always gone by then. But for some strange reason, she was still in the rectory." The secretary recognized Jennie's former name, and although she didn't know the name of the Kogovseks' hotel, she did know that Gene was attending a meeting of a fraternal organization. The secretary called a local member of the organization—who is never home on Saturdays—and he called one of Gene's sons, who is never home on Saturdays. Somehow, all calls connected on the first try, and within minutes word had spread among the extended family, back to the parish secretary, back to the hospital, and, ultimately, to Gene at his hotel.

The Angola hospital, however, was not equipped to handle Jennie's severe brain injury, and, because a storm was approaching, by the time Gene got to the hospital they had already airlifted Jennie to a hospital in Fort Wayne, Indiana. They gave Gene a plastic bag of Jennie's belongings. He drove the forty miles without a hitch and immediately found the hospital, although he had never been in Fort Wayne. The news was grim: Jennie had already received a CT scan, and Gene had one of two choices to make. "I could do nothing, and Jennie would die before morning. Or the surgeon could operate to relieve the pressure on Jennie's brain, and see what happened next." Gene felt Jennie would want a chance for life. And so, just six scant hours after she was found, Jennie's surgery was completed. The prognosis was not good, but by now the entire extended family had arrived. They pinned a scapular (a pair of small cloth squares worn on a string under the clothing that symbolize an aspect of faith, such as Christ's passion or Mary's sorrows) to Jennie's head bandages, and the prayer power began.

Little signs and blessings continued to come. When Gene asked hospital personnel if they could recommend a nearby hotel, they offered him the last room in the former student nurses' quarters, which would certainly make expenses easier to bear. Directly across the street was St. Jude's Catholic Church, with its perpetual adoration chapel. (St. Jude is known as the patron saint of impossible causes.) Gene spent a great part of every day there, with comfort wrapping its warmth around him. When he eventually returned home he opened the large plastic bag of Jennie's belongings. "Mixed in with her clothes was a lady's blood-stained jacket that had been under Jennie's head, and the outer wrap that had protected her from the rain." It began to dawn on him how blessed Jennie had been to have people available to help her right away. What if she had had the stroke in a more deserted area?

Jennie eventually transferred to a hospital near their home, and upon her first examination there, a physician cautioned the family that Jennie would probably never walk again. "Later, he was present when the nurses got Jennie up for the first time since her stroke," Gene says, "and he watched her take her first steps." The doctor was pale. But perhaps he had forgotten the power of prayer.

Today, Jennie wears a brace on her left leg and cannot use her left arm very well, but the rest of her is perfect, and she and Gene enjoy a rich and busy life. "We have been back to Fremont several times since this happened," Gene says. "We have talked to the mall manager and a number of mall employees who were working when Jennie had the stroke. We have even advertised at the mall and in local newspapers. But despite our best efforts, we have been unable to find the two women who helped Jennie that day." The couple is convinced they were her guardian angels. Their garments, cleaned and pressed, remain in Gene's closet at home.

PATRICIA'S VALENTINE

The golden moments in the stream of life rush past us,
and we see nothing but sand; the angels come to visit us,
and we only know them when they are gone.

—GEORGE ELIOT

The valentines in the window displays seemed to mock Judy Kimball as she sloshed through the drugstore parking lot in Kent, Washington. As others demonstrated their love, she felt only loneliness and heartbreak. She glanced at passersby, all seemingly deep into their own thoughts. Other people's marriages failed, she knew, and somehow they went on living. But how? It had been only six days since her husband had told her he wanted a divorce, six days since her life had taken on a surreal feeling, and grief threatened to overwhelm her.

She hadn't expected anything like this to happen. They'd been together almost nineteen years, and she thought those had been happy years. But now she wondered how much of her husband's supposed contentment had been a lie. He had explained little, just gotten his things together and left while she and their three children reeled, trying to grasp what was happening. She hadn't shared the news with anyone yet, nor had she even cried. The hurt was too wrenching for talk or tears.

The first few days had passed in a blur. Somehow Judy summoned up the composure to cancel a dinner party she and her husband had planned to host on Saturday; she said that all three children had come down with the flu. And then there was her Wednesday night class in fiction writing. Now that the kids were older, she'd felt it was her turn to follow a long-held dream, to write, publish, and share any successes with her husband.

But now that dream was dead. She had skipped last week's class, and would probably drop out. What was the point? She had obviously failed at one of her most important tasks—being a beloved wife—so why should she expect success in any other aspect of her life? This trip to the drugstore for valentines for her children was the first time she'd ventured out all week, and it was taking its toll. She felt shaky and ill.

"Judy!" She heard the call from across the parking lot, and turned. Waving at her was Patricia, another student in her fiction writing class, wearing the same Black Watch plaid cape she always did. Judy waved back, hoping Patricia wouldn't come any closer. She seemed nice, but Judy didn't feel up to talking to anyone. Within seconds however, Patricia was at her side. "Hey, we missed you at class last week," she said, concern in her eyes. "Are you all right?"

The tears began to come. "My—my husband has asked for a separation—and ultimately a divorce. He's moved out." Judy was astonished at her own words. Patricia was nothing more than a casual acquaintance, someone who sat in the back of the classroom and occasionally smiled at her. Why was Judy sharing something so personal with her?

But the compassion on Patricia's face was real. "Come on. It's chilly out here. Let's talk in my car." She guided Judy to a nearby vehicle.

The car seemed a warm and safe oasis, and Judy wept as she poured out her hurt, anger, and fear. Hadn't she tried, as best she knew how, to honor her commitment, to be the woman God wanted her to be? Why then, had he let this terrible thing happen to her and their precious children? She looked at Patricia and was shocked to see tears running down *her* cheeks. She shouldn't be putting this nice woman through this. She didn't even know if Patricia believed in God. "I'm so sorry to burden you with this," she whispered as her sobbing wound down. "You could never understand."

Patricia laid a hand on Judy's arm. "You're wrong," she said softly. "I do understand." Swiftly she removed something from her black cape and dropped it into Judy's hand. It was an angel pin.

"God hasn't forgotten you, Judy," Patricia said gently. "He just has other plans for you. You will survive this. Trust me."

"Thank you." Judy gave Patricia a quick hug and then slipped from the car. She was still shaky, but inside her—glowing as if for the first time—was a little flicker of hope. She closed her fingers around the angel pin and remembered the Lord's faithful promise, "I will never forsake you or abandon you" (Hebrews 13:5). She, who had always relied on her husband, was going to lean on God's strength now.

On the following Wednesday, Judy returned to her fiction class. It had taken a bit of interior pushing, but it was important that she make a beginning. And she knew Patricia, her newfound friend, would cheer her on. However, Patricia was absent. Nor did she come the next week, or the next. If only Judy had thought to get her last name or telephone number! Class records were private, but on the following Wednesday, Judy approached the teacher. "Remember Patricia, the woman in the Black Watch plaid cape?" she asked.

The teacher looked mystified.

"She sat in the back of class," Judy added. "She hasn't been here the past few weeks, and I'd like to contact her."

The teacher shook her head. "I don't remember any woman in a plaid cape."

"Her first name was Patricia," Judy persisted. "If you can give me her last name . . ."

The teacher ran her finger down the class roster, then looked at Judy. "There's no Patricia enrolled in this class," she said. "And no one by that name has dropped out."

"Pat? Patty? Tricia?"

The instructor shook her head. "Sorry. I wish I could help, but I'm afraid not."

Judy stood in a daze. *You will survive this,* Patricia had told her. Maybe Patricia had never been there for class. Maybe she had been there only for Judy. It was a mystery, but isn't life filled with them?

Judy sat down at her desk and reached for her notebook. She had a story to write.

THE LEAST OF THESE

Oh, there's nothing on earth half so holy
As the innocent heart of a child!

—"THE CHILDREN," CHARLES MONROE DICKINSON

Andrea Martin has always felt a strong connection between herself and her little goddaughter Katie. "Her mother, Amanda, is my cousin, and we are also very close," Andrea says. "But right from the day Katie was born, I felt a special bond." As she grew, one of the unusual things about Katie was her occasional comment about a little boy she sometimes saw. "Who are you waving to?" Andrea would ask her.

"The *boy,* Aunt Andrea!" Katie would respond, as if everyone could see him. It would have been simple to suppose he was an imaginary companion, which the typical preschooler will conjure up during playtime. But on more than one occasion, Katie's mother, Amanda, had caught a glimpse of a little boy in Katie's room. Who was he? Amanda hadn't said much about this vision, until her father reported the same phenomenon. Both continued to catch an occasional glimpse of the boy, who always hovered around Katie's room.

When Katie was about three, Amanda became pregnant with her second child. When she was almost ready to give birth, her friends, including Andrea, took her out for dinner at a Mexican restaurant. Because it was a special event, Katie was included. "We thought the spicy foods might speed up Amanda's delivery!" Andrea says. Even if it did, there would be no problem—Andrea had promised to stay overnight at the house, so in case anything happened in the night, she would be there to care for Katie.

The women talked and laughed and had a wonderful time. Andrea noticed that Katie seemed enthralled with the red helium balloons that were bobbing from the ceiling and wafting over the tables in the restaurant. When the dinner was over, Andrea bought a balloon for Katie. The little girl was thrilled. She clung to it in the car.

But when everyone entered the house, just for a moment, Katie let go of the balloon, and it sailed away, up to the high cathedral ceiling in the living room. Katie burst into tears. "The living room ceiling was at least two stories high and kind of closed in," Andrea says. "There was no way any of us could reach that balloon. I felt so bad for Katie. I hadn't meant to make her cry." Knowing how important such things are to little children, Andrea tucked Katie into bed and gave her extra hugs.

Despite the Mexican food, no baby arrived that night, and the following morning, Andrea was the first one to get up. She walked past Katie's open door and stopped in surprise. It couldn't be. But there, bobbing cheerfully against the eight-foot ceiling was the red balloon. Andrea went into the room and stared at it, amazed. How had the balloon traveled from the high living-room ceiling, down the narrow eight-foot-high hallway, and into Katie's low-ceilinged bedroom? It was still round and full and obviously hadn't lost any of its helium. She looked over at the bed, where Katie was lying, awake and smiling. "Honey, how did this balloon get into your room?"

Katie smiled. "I asked the boy."

"The boy?"

Katie nodded. "You know, Aunt Andrea. The boy who waves to me sometimes. I was sad because the balloon was so high. So I asked the boy to get it for me, and he did."

Just like a guardian angel. Andrea was getting chills. No request was too small for heaven. And wasn't a balloon the perfect symbol of love?

Recently, Katie was a junior bridesmaid in Andrea's wedding. And although she hasn't mentioned him in a few years, everyone believes that "the boy" attended, too.

113

People who work to develop children's spiritual natures all agree that, like Katie, many of them seem to have a pipeline to heaven. Because children are vulnerable and sinless, they can often pray far more effectively and innocently than we, their elders, can. But unless we help them to develop this gift, it will be unused.

Peggy Dale, of Indianapolis, Indiana, had never thought about asking a small child to pray for anything important. Then her daughter Julie developed a health problem. Julie was already a walking miracle. Like her sister and one of her brothers, she had diabetes, and many of the severe complications it brings, including blindness. Yet Julie's sunny, outgoing personality attracted and inspired everyone she met. Julie had a happy marriage and was involved in many activities; except for occasional treatment for problems stemming from her diabetes, she had managed to live a relatively normal life. Then, in 2004, she had an operation. "It should have been fairly routine," Peggy explains, "but afterward, the doctors discovered that Julie had a small hole in her intestine."

This was a very serious situation for Julie. Fifteen years before, she had received a kidney and a pancreas transplant, and both organs were functioning very well. However, due to her anti-rejection medication, Julie's veins were exceptionally tiny. Now, in order for Julie to get nourishment, the doctors had to bypass her intestine and feed her intravenously. But the thick feeding liquid, unable to go through her veins, collected in her left side and caused extreme swelling. The feedings had to be discontinued.

What should be done? The doctors were certain that, left alone, the hole would probably close itself within two to three months. But Julie couldn't eat, could only drink small sips of water, and would die of starvation by then! As the first few days passed, and her physicians tried to come up with an answer, Julie got hungrier, and Peggy began to panic.

"I was at the hospital every day at that point," Peggy says. "And eventually I brought a book from home to read, *The Power of Miracles,* a gift one of my grandsons had given me at Christmas. It had been lying around for a while, since it wasn't my usual reading fare." One of the chapters talked about the importance of teaching young children to lay hands on people who were sick. Peggy read the chapter twice. Then she phoned her great-grandson, eight-year-old Jacob.

At Peggy's house, people talk about God and pray occasionally, so Jacob was used to that environment. But this was a little different. "Would you come to the hospital with Great-Grandpa tonight, to visit Aunt Julie?" Peggy asked. Jacob's mother would drop him off at Peggy's house.

"Sure!" Like everyone else, Jacob loved Aunt Julie. Peggy decided not to mention anything more until Jacob arrived. She didn't want him to change his mind.

That night, however, when Jacob arrived, Peggy drew him aside. "Jacob, would you do something special for Aunt Julie tonight at the hospital? Would you lay your hands on her stomach and ask God to heal her? You can say it any way you want to."

Jacob was completely agreeable even though, to Peggy's knowledge, he had never done anything like this before. She watched her husband and Jacob walk out to the car while she whispered a prayer of her own.

Later that evening when her husband returned, Peggy was eager to hear what, if anything, Jacob had done. And she was not disappointed. Jacob had gone over to Julie's hospital bed and said, "Aunt Julie, do you mind if I pray for you?"

"Of course not, honey."

Then Jacob gently laid his small hands on Julie's stomach. "Dear God," his clear voice rang out, "please heal my Aunt Julie, and make her tummy better."

That was it. Nothing complicated or difficult. Just the simple prayer of an innocent child. Even if nothing happened, Peggy would be satisfied.

But something did happen. During a routine test the following week, it was discovered that the hole in Julie's intestine had completely closed. It had not taken two to three months after all. In fact, it might have happened at the very moment Jacob asked. No one will ever know for sure; even the doctors who were surprised, if not stunned.

Julie went home and recovered from her surgery. And Jacob? Who knows how many more times he will pray over someone—because on that one occasion someone simply asked him to do it. If you have young children in your family, be sure to ask them, too. It's a special way of praying—with blessed results.

Helpers on the Highway

Friends are kisses blown to us by angels.
—Author Unknown

Debbie Core's friend Doris Marshall was scheduled for open-heart surgery in February of 2004. The women had been friends for more than thirty years. "We met when both of us were working for a nursing home," Debbie says. "Doris was fifteen years older than I, and she had a lot of heartache in her life, but she was funny and wonderful to be around. And she made the best apple dumplings I ever ate!" Eventually the women each moved on to other jobs, but they continued their close friendship. "I stayed with her in the hospital the night before the surgery," Debbie says. "We talked all night, and we prayed together. Doris said that if she didn't make it, she was ready for the angels to take her home to God." Debbie didn't want to consider that possibility. She wanted to share many more years with Doris.

The surgery was a success, and a few days later Debbie visited Doris again. All seemed to be going well, except that Doris felt exceptionally cold, especially in her hands. "Here," Debbie said, reaching into her coat pocket, "you can have my gloves."

"No," Doris protested, "it's cold out—you'll need them." Actually, she was right. Debbie had chronic car trouble, especially with her brakes. She was always expecting her old clunker to break down and leave her stranded somewhere in bad weather, without wheels or the money to repair the wheels. But now she waved aside Doris's protests and put the gloves on her friend's hands. "They were stretchy-type gloves I had just bought from the Dollar Store, no big deal. I was glad I could do something for her." The women talked and laughed some more, and then Debbie went home. It was the last time they were together. Doris died suddenly a few days later.

Debbie was devastated. She went to the funeral, but even the rendition of one of her favorite songs, "Serenaded by Angels," was not enough to comfort her. What would life without Doris be like? She thought back to their conversation on the night before surgery, how Doris had said she was ready to meet God if this was the right time. Had the angels come? Was Doris in heaven? How could Debbie know for sure?

The days seemed to drag without Doris. And late winter always seemed gloomy. One day, Debbie's car almost stopped running, so she dropped it off at the repair shop. Soon the mechanic phoned Debbie at work. "Are you sitting down?" he asked.

"Yes," Debbie answered. "Why?"

"Because you'll be shocked when I tell you that you had only about 30 percent of your brakes still functioning, and one of the belts is cracked, and . . ." He continued with a litany of problems, any one of which could have caused a major accident, and Debbie had been very lucky to avoid one. She knew it was more than that. She praised and thanked God. He had surely been looking out for her.

God, and perhaps her best friend. "I picked up the car that afternoon, got in behind the wheel, and drove away," Debbie says. "It was running so beautifully, and I started to praise God again." Then, from the corner of her eye, she saw something lying on the floor. At the next red light, she leaned over to pick it up and discovered that it was a pair of black gloves—*her* stretchy black gloves from the Dollar Store, the ones she had put on Doris's cold hands that last night. Debbie had never thought to try to retrieve them from the hospital. But how had they gotten here, inside her car?

"I have thought about it," she says today, "and I am sure that an angel put those gloves in my car. I had helped another person—just as the Bible asks us to do. And I think God was letting me know that as I helped Doris, he helped me." Perhaps it was a signal from Doris, too, to let her friend know that she was home, safe in God's arms.

Debbie has a better car now, and has adjusted, just a little, to life without her best friend. But she keeps the black gloves in her glove compartment, a constant reminder of God's care.

Cars seem to be involved in many angel stories. Perhaps it's because we spend so much time in them today, and angels must be where we are! Many people make it a habit to pray briefly right before they turn on the ignition, to bless and protect themselves and those they'll meet on the road.

Joe and Mary Prendergast of Marlton, New Jersey, are both musicians. They established a music school in Merchantville, New Jersey, in 1960. Mary taught piano, and Joe, piano and voice. As if they weren't busy enough, their family ultimately included six daughters and three sons (and, they both agree, many guardian angels to be there when Mom or Dad couldn't be). Joe took added jobs with a band and was also the music director at a local church. During those busy years, as real-estate taxes continued to go up, the family gave up their original house and lived in the music school. "You do what you have to do when there are nine children," Joe points out.

It had long been a dream of the Prendergasts to have a vacation home in the Pocono Mountains of Pennsylvania, a place where their children could spread out, make noise, ski, and enjoy the pleasures of nature. However, they had all but given up trying to find something affordable until a friend recommended Wagner's Forest on Pocono Lake. Joe and Mary visited the area the following weekend and found two perfect lots. It took almost three years (and plenty of hands) to build their wonderful A-frame home, but everyone agreed that it was a dream come true.

The family enjoyed the home immensely, but it was an expensive luxury, and as time went by, they needed some extra income to keep up with the rising overhead costs. Renting to vacationers when they weren't using the house themselves seemed like a logical solution. After the tenants left, Joe and Mary would drive the three-hour trip to clean the house and make any necessary repairs. Occasionally, Joe went alone.

People usually rented during the summertime but frequently came to ski, too. On a clear Sunday night at about 10:30 p.m., Joe decided to drive to the house to clean up after the latest tenants. "Joe, that's not a good idea," Mary protested. "You know your night vision is becoming a problem. Why don't we both go early tomorrow instead?"

"I want to start first thing in the morning so I can get back here soon," Joe said. "I'll be fine." Mary wasn't happy, but she said nothing more. Angels would accompany him. They always did.

About midnight, however, Joe began to feel drowsy. Traffic on the Pennsylvania turnpike was sparse, but he knew it wouldn't be wise to continue. He was approaching a small rest area where a semitruck was parked, so he pulled behind the semi, turned off the engine, and promptly fell asleep. "At about 1:00 a.m. the driver of the semi started its engine, which awakened me," Joe says. "I felt fine, so I resumed my journey." Soon he saw the familiar roadside sign ahead: "Allentown, next exit to the right." It was the last thing he remembered . . .

. . . until he awakened, midway through the Lehigh Tunnel. He was traveling at exactly thirty-five miles per hour in the middle of the right lane—and was staring, not at the road, but downward at his thighs "That meant that for fifteen miles, sound asleep, I had navigated a road through mountainous terrain, with many twists and turns. And I had not even been looking at the road."

Now, instead of stopping, Joe gently accelerated to about fifty-five miles an hour, since he was still on the turnpike. Everything seemed normal. Perhaps another driver had seen him driving erratically and had awakened Joe by blowing his horn. But there was no one behind or in front of him. He looked at the dashboard. Still plenty of gas—but the dashboard clock told the story. It was 1:45 a.m. For the past half hour his guardian angel had taken the wheel while Joe slept.

"Anyone would think that I would have been excited and trembling," Joe says, "but I wasn't. I was completely calm, although bewildered and surprised that I was still alive. I drove for another hour with complete assurance until I reached Pocono Lake."

Why did this happen? Joe is not sure. "It was clearly not my time to die, and God had his reasons to spare me." He has told many people about this adventure, "and those with faith have no trouble understanding what occurred."

Diane Harrington, of Milwaukie, Oregon, had just lost her job. Money would be very tight for a while, so she asked God to watch over her in a special way during this difficult time. Diane had some documents to drop off at her former employer's office, so she drove to CopyMax to prepare them, then drove into the city to deliver everything. Pulling into a parking place, she reached into her purse for her wallet to grab change for the parking meter.

There was no wallet in her purse.

Oh, no. *Stay calm,* she told herself, taking a deep breath. The wallet had been in her purse at CopyMax. But she needed to deliver these documents now, and without change for the meter, she was risking a thirty-five dollar ticket. Just then, Diane realized that it was Sunday, hence no meter charge. Whew! She hurried into the building and left the material at the office door. Then she drove hastily back to CopyMax, hoping that someone had turned in the wallet.

"The CopyMax store is on a hillside," Diane explains, "and its parking lot slopes down to a major traffic thoroughfare. There is a bank directly below the store, and usually, the lot is very full. I found a spot close to the door of CopyMax, at the top of the hill." Diane entered the store and immediately saw her wallet behind the counter on a table. Relief flooded her, even more so when she discovered that her money was still in it. Giving thanks to this unknown Good Samaritan, she thanked the store personnel, put her wallet in her purse, and went out to her car.

The car was not there.

This was not turning out to be a good day. Refusing to become hysterical (yet), Diane asked other shoppers if anyone had seen the car. "A 1997 Ford Contour, taupe color, parked *right here*." No one had seen anything. "Cars can be easily hot-wired and stolen today," remarked one passerby, which did nothing to stem Diane's rising anxiety. What if the car was trashed, and her insurance didn't cover all of it? By then, nearly everyone at the mall must have known her car was missing, yet no one had a clue. She went back into CopyMax and phoned the police to report a stolen vehicle.

But while still on the phone, Diane noticed a couple hurrying into the store, their faces wreathed in smiles. "Your car is not stolen," the man called to her. "Come out and see this."

Diane followed them outside. They led her across the parking lot, and on and on. Why were they going so far away? If her car wasn't stolen, then where was it? Suddenly, Diane caught sight of her Ford, way in the distance, in the middle of *another* parking lot.

It looked completely undamaged. But how had it gotten all the way over there?

The couple laughed. "You had to see it to believe it!" the woman said. "Your car rolled down the hill, swerved around the bank and the other cars in the lot, exited at the driveway, rolled across four lanes of traffic, then over an embankment at the Jack in the Box restaurant, hit a little tree, and finally ended up in *that* parking lot."

"We saw it happening and came back here to find the owner," the man added. Diane was stunned. All that rolling, and no collisions? No one injured, no property damaged except that one tree? Diane thanked the couple and went inside the Jack in the Box to find the manager and report the damaged tree.

"I'll pay for it," she assured him, thinking of her pinched budget, but he shook his head. "It was a little tree, just planted," he said, "and you are safe, and that's all that matters."

His customers, too, had seen the car moving along. "It was incredible," one woman reported to Diane. "Your car went peacefully around every obstacle, almost as if someone were driving it!"

By now a police officer had arrived and was checking the runaway car. Like the others, he shook his head in disbelief. "I can't see any reason to give you a ticket, ma'am," he said. "Just be careful."

"I will," she assured him. She would be very careful, and before she started for home, she would take a moment to thank God. For truly, he had sent an angel to drive her car through this amazing obstacle course, had brought kind and honest people to help her, and had shielded her from both physical and financial harm. If God loved her enough to do this for her, he would surely find her the right job, too. She felt a smile coming from her toes all the way through her spirit as she turned the key in the ignition.

Lost and Found

Angels are constantly asked to locate lost objects. And the ways in which they solve these problems are often unique. Barbara Brabec knows this. She is the acknowledged "guru" of the home-based business crowd, a popular author and Internet expert. She is smart and organized—but like many busy women, she is also in a hurry most of the time. One gusty spring Saturday, Barbara hurried out the door to run a few errands. "I had cashed in a $2000 IRA and received the check this past week, and had a couple of other small checks for deposit, so I'd written the slip and endorsed the checks at home," she says. "In the garage, my hands full, I laid the three paper-clipped checks on the roof of the car so I could get my keys out and put other stuff down on the front seat." Barbara got in the car, tore out of the driveway and was almost at the bank drive-in before she realized she had left the checks on the roof of the car!

On a windy day like today, with dead leaves and papers whipping around, they could be anywhere! Turning around to go home again, Barbara cried and prayed. "Logic told me I didn't have a chance of finding those checks," she says, "but fools always have hope." As she turned onto her street, she began looking at lawns for bits and pieces of paper. Nothing resembled her precious packet.

Then Barbara realized something else. She had endorsed the checks without writing "For deposit only," on them, because she was just going to hand them to the bank teller. But now any unscrupulous person could find her IRA check and cash it. Since it was Saturday, there was no way she could notify the company to stop payment on it. She really needed this money—and it was as good as gone.

Barbara swerved into her driveway, and her heart almost stopped. Lying motionless on the sidewalk near the garage door—in the midst of blustery wind gusts—were her three paper-clipped checks. Barbara screeched to a halt, leaped out of the car and grabbed them. "I knew God had sent my guardian angel to put his foot on them and hold them there," she says, "because there was NO WAY they wouldn't have blown away otherwise."

It had been a while since Barbara had received a miracle, but this was a big one. She cried again, this time tears of gratitude to God as she drove back to the bank, a little more slowly this time.

And today she wants "to SHOUT to the world that God is good, and he does watch out for us, especially when we forget things!"

Reverend Monsignor Frank Korba would agree. By his own admission, the pastor of St. Nicholas Byzantine Catholic Church in Munster, Indiana, had never thought much about angels until a parishioner lent him a copy of *Where Angels Walk.* He read it from cover to cover and was fascinated. A few weeks later, he had a chance to make his very first request of angels.

St. Nicholas, like most churches, has a parishioner who handles much of the finances, paying the bills and making bank deposits. And each year, like other churches, St. Nicholas takes up a stewardship collection for their diocese, which is centered in Parma, Ohio. That year, the collection was taken up as usual, but the volunteer was leaving the next day on vacation. So he dropped in on Father Frank Sunday night. "Inside this envelope is twelve hundred dollars in cash and about nine hundred dollars in checks from the collection," he told Father Frank. "Tomorrow, take it all to the bank, ask them to total it and give you a check for the entire amount. Then send the check in this envelope to the diocese." Father Frank looked at the open envelope. It was bulging with checks and cash and was already addressed to the diocese and stamped. "You've made it very easy for me," he told the man. "Have a wonderful time on your vacation!"

The following morning, Father Frank gathered all his mail, including the thick envelope, and set out on his walk. It was a few hours later before it dawned on him that he had dropped *all* the mail in a nearby mailbox, including the open envelope, stuffed with cash and checks! He was panic-stricken. He went immediately to church and knelt before his Lord. It was then that he remembered that there were angels in church, as well. "God," he prayed, "please send your angels to that envelope, wherever it is. May they form protection around it so that nothing falls out or is destroyed. Please return it safely." He had never asked for something so unusual. Of course he believed in miracles but he had never asked for one quite like this.

Heart pounding, he left the church and went to the Munster post office. "Is there any way I can check the mail from that box?" he asked. "I threw something in that I shouldn't have."

"Happens all the time," the clerk acknowledged. "But that box has already been emptied, Father."

Oh, no. Father Frank envisioned money flying around as the postal worker opened the mailbox, or checks lying loose at the bottom. "What should I do now?" he asked.

"You can call the Gary post office. That's where it would be sorted."

Father Frank did. But the sorted mail had already left Gary to be transferred to Cleveland, and from there, finally, to Parma. And why would he think that it would still be intact? Surely those huge sorting machines would have already scattered its contents—and how many hands would have handled the cash? He went about his work that day with a heavy heart. He would somehow have to make up the total of that collection from his own stretched budget, to say nothing of the missing checks, which would have to be stopped or reissued. All day he hoped that someone would call—perhaps a postal worker or even an honest citizen—to let him know that at least some of the material had been recovered. But the phone didn't ring. By evening, Father Frank realized that he must alert the diocesan office and begin the difficult task of letting parishioners know how careless he had been.

The following morning, he phoned the secretary at the Parma office. "Mary, something has happened," he blurted, before she could speak. "I mailed an envelope that wasn't supposed to be mailed—"

"It's okay," Mary interrupted. "It came today. I'm holding it right now."

"What? It's already there?"

"With a lot of cash in it. And checks, too."

Father Frank's head spun. "Is . . . is it *open?*"

"Well, you couldn't seal it. It's much too thick for that."

It was impossible. And yet hadn't he asked the angels for a miracle? No, even more specific than that, hadn't he asked them to form protection around the envelope so nothing would fall out? Evidently, the heavenly host had done just that.

When word got out, one St. Nicholas parishioner was heard to jest that perhaps all collection money should be kept away from Father Frank in the future. But the rest of the congregation took the event with the sense of awe and gratitude that often accompanies angelic intervention. "Ask and you shall receive," is no idle promise. Not to those who believe.

PART 3

MIRACLES OF KINDNESS

LIFE THAT GROWS FROM LOVE

Faith is not believing that God can. It is knowing that God will.

—BEN STEIN

Regi Sue Smith* would agree with the above statement. Her beautiful attitude about life must have been nourished by the angels who brought her through some truly dark moments.

Regi was a teenage bride, and a mother by her eighteenth birthday. At nineteen, she had already divorced, and by twenty-one she had been diagnosed with cervical cancer. What a start on life! Regi loved children and had wanted more, but it was not going to be. The next several years were difficult, as she worked at low-paying jobs and went through several surgeries. "There were times when I walked to work because I didn't have money for gas," she says. "But

* last name changed

Kenny kept me going. I felt that God had given me this little child, and God would help me provide for him."

As time passed, things began to look more hopeful. Regi celebrated her thirtieth birthday cancer free. Two years later she met the man of her dreams, John Smith. "He had never been married, and had no children. And although by now I had been well for several years, he knew we would be unable to have any children together." It was a sorrow for both of them, but they accepted the situation.

Shortly after the wedding, Regi's brother became terminally ill. So Regi, John, and Kenny, now a teenager, decided to move to Florida to help and support the family. By the time Regi's brother died, everyone had put down roots in the area, and they decided to stay. Regi, still wanting a life involving children, decided to open a home-based day care for newborns to five year olds in temporary protective custody—that is, children in foster care who were scheduled to be returned to their parents when the adults finished drug and/or alcohol rehab. "It was both wonderful and heartbreaking to work with these children," Regi recalls. "The hardest part was releasing them to go back to abusive families. Many would return to protective services again and again."

Social workers soon noticed that Regi seemed to have a special knack for handling these children and for preventing them from lapsing into depression. Her service was unique in that she provided day care around the clock. ("Having been a single mom, I knew there were times when women just had to work late or deal with an emergency.") At one point, four preschoolers were staying overnight with her regularly, and she also offered weekend care. "It got hectic at times. My assistant arrived in the early afternoon, and John was there to help in the evenings. Our weekend outings always included one or more extra kids, but we didn't mind at all. We became very attached to all of them."

One morning, Regi was asked to go to a women's shelter and observe a ten-month-old boy born addicted to crack cocaine and thus developmentally delayed. Could she consider becoming his foster mother? Regi had never been a foster parent. "And Ivan cried *all* the time. But there was something in his eyes when he looked at me." She agreed to try.

Ivan lived with Regi and John for at least six months before his birth mother was permitted to see him. By this time he had learned that there was no need for him to cry. Instead, he was walking, learning words, and smiling. The mother began her once-a-week visits with her son. "The visits were only three hours long," Regi says, "but Ivan always came back filthy, and of course, crying again." How could she stand by and watch Ivan's hard-won gains evaporate? God had always been with her as she cared for these special children, but now she prayed even harder that, in some way, this little boy would be saved.

And soon her prayers were heard. Ivan's mother went on another drug binge, and she realized that Ivan would be taken away from her again at her next court date. She contacted Regi. "I'm not a good mother for Ivan," she admitted. "I'll lose him eventually anyway, so . . . would you want to adopt him?"

Regi was dumbfounded. She had never allowed herself to dream of adopting any of the children in her care; all of them belonged to someone else. But she and John loved Ivan, and if he were to have any chance at life, it would have to come through parents like them. They contacted a lawyer, and Ivan became their son.

Just a short time later, another mother dropped her sad-eyed eleven-month-old daughter, Brandi, off at Regi's day care. "Just for a couple of weeks," the mother promised. "I need some time to get straightened out."

The birth mother never returned, and eventually Regi and John adopted this baby, too.

"Brandi looked exactly like a Cabbage Patch Kid—so cute—but at first the only one she would communicate with was Ivan," Regi remembers. "As I rocked her and sang to her, she eventually started to respond with smiles and giggles. Soon she was like a daily dose of sunshine." Between two adorable toddlers and Kenny, the doting older brother, Regi and John had the perfect family.

As it turned out, all Ivan and Brandi had needed was love. Today, Regi is proud of the bright and happy young adults they have become, and she is still thankful to God for finding them for her. For wasn't there a purpose for all of this, even the most difficult times? "From the beginning of time, God knew that there would eventually be two babies that would need us as their parents, and he led us to them. Had I not had cancer, I probably would have had a much different life, one without John or the babies. In its own way, my illness was a blessing."

Today, Regi struggles with rheumatoid arthritis in her back, but she has the joy of Kenny's children to delight her each day. Always the darkness as part of the light; it is that way for all of us until we reach our destiny. But in the meantime we can choose to live in despair or, with women like Regi lighting the way, in joy.

ANGEL ON THE TELEPHONE

Do not pray for tasks equal to your powers.
Pray for power equal to your tasks.

—PHILLIPS BROOKS

It had been a busy day at the San Jose, California, police and fire communications center. Keao Mai, a dispatcher, was glad to get home and relax. She was grateful that the 911 system was in place and that she could help so many troubled people, and she was especially pleased when she could send police officers home safely to their families at the end of a shift. Despite a natural shyness, Keao could find the humor in any situation and often relieved workplace tension by making her coworkers laugh. She was organized, too. "We could always tell where 'K' had worked her last shift," says fellow dispatcher Susan Blair, "because all her maps and books were right at your fingertips when you used that space after her, and you could find anything you needed." But stress at this type of job was inevitable, and Keao knew that downtime was crucial.

On this particular evening, Keao's roommate, Angela, also a police dispatcher, was busy with chores, so Keao threw on one of her favorite oversized tie-dyed shirts, mixed up a batch of cookie dough, put it in to bake, and turned the television on to her favorite sitcom rerun. At last, peace and quiet.

She had just started to relax when the phone rang. Keao was tempted to ignore it. But something nudged her, and she picked it up. "Hello?"

The woman's voice on the other end was trembling and somewhat faint. "I—I think I'm going to shoot myself."

Keao was instantly alert, her fatigue forgotten. "Why would you want to do that?" she asked, keeping her voice casual and friendly, as she had been trained to do on her job.

"No one understands." The woman on the other end started to cry. "My husband . . . the kids . . . no one cares."

Keao had handled suicide calls, but always at work. Now she was at home with no reinforcements—no fellow dispatchers to back her up, no transfer buttons or resource book or extra phone lines. Nor did she have caller ID, and the kitchen phone wasn't portable. Angela was in her bedroom, too far away to be summoned without alerting the caller. With a sinking heart, Keao realized that she was completely alone.

Well, not exactly alone. God was here, wasn't he? *God, help me help her.* "Why don't you tell me about it?" she asked softly. "Maybe I can help."

As Keao tapped a pencil loudly against a kitchen counter, hoping to attract Angela's attention, the weeping caller told a familiar story, one of loneliness, a longing for appreciation and love. If people only knew how easy it was to care for one another, Keao thought. Just a hug, a word of forgiveness—it would make every day holy. But this woman seemed intent on shooting herself. Several times, Keao changed the subject, hoping to calm the caller and get her telephone number. Her hands, gripping the receiver, turned sweaty. The cookies began to burn. *God, help,* she prayed. The caller couldn't take her own life! Keao was already forming a bond with her. "Where are you from?" she asked, to keep the woman talking.

"Hilo, in Hawaii."

Keao was astonished. "*I'm* from Hilo!" she exclaimed.

"You're Hawaiian? This is amazing!"

It was the opening Keao needed. "Look, why don't you give me your telephone number, just in case we get cut off? I'd like to call you back and talk more about Hilo. Maybe we have friends in common."

"Well . . ." The caller trusted Keao now. Slowly she recited her number.

Just then, Angela wandered into the kitchen, no doubt checking out the smell of burnt cookies coming from the oven. Keao motioned frantically to the receiver, then handed the pad with the telephone number on it to Angela. Using a cell phone, Angela alerted a rescue unit, which sped to the caller's house. In just a few moments, Keao heard people talking on the other end of the phone and paramedic sirens in the background. Someone confiscated the gun and led the woman out to the ambulance. Someone else hung up the phone. Keao whispered a silent prayer of thanks. Maybe the woman would find the help she needed. Perhaps Keao would follow through and visit her.

It was a full day later when it occurred to Keao that the woman claimed to have dialed 911. How, then, had she reached the home telephone of a rescue worker from Hilo, who knew just what to do?

Keao knows that this was no coincidence. With God and his angels, nothing (not even crossed telephone wires) is impossible.[1]

The Ten Percent Solution

Bring the whole tithe

    into the storehouse, . . .

    and try me in this, says the LORD of hosts:

Shall I not open for you the floodgates of heaven,

    to pour down blessing upon you without measure?

            —MALACHI 3:10–11

Serving God almost always involves going against the grain. Often, the sacrifices or decisions we are called upon to make just don't seem sensible to people outside our faith community. But these may be the very moments that, if we choose God's way, can bring about the greatest blessings.

So it was with Clark Cothern. The son of a Southern Baptist pastor, Clark grew up vowing he would never be one. "Not because my parents weren't terrific," he says, "but I saw the heartache that is part of helping so many hurting people," and he wanted no part of it. Instead, Clark prepared for a career in music.

During his first year of college, he took a job in a small Phoenix, Arizona, church as a part-time music director. Later, he toured the United States and northern Europe with a singing group, and he saw many different styles of churches and leadership. "I had thought my dad was an exception, but this trip showed me that there were plenty of 'normal' people in the ministry," he says. He also noticed that people in need were coming to him for advice and prayer. Clark didn't feel that his prayers were any more significant than anyone else's, but he did the best he could to deal with the people who came to him for help. Then he got married, and with his wife Joy's support, served in several churches, usually as a music minister. After the birth of their second baby, the couple settled down in Ann Arbor, Michigan, not far from Joy's family. It was there that Clark's desire to become a pastor grew.

"Maybe it was the positive response I received from that wonderful congregation," he says, "or maybe it was just God's voice, nudging me to follow where he had been leading me all along." But one day Clark announced to Joy that not only did he believe he should be a pastor, but he should start a new church—in a place where people didn't usually attend church.

Joy was supportive of the idea, so she and Clark attended conferences, read books, and talked with others who had served as home missionaries. Ironically, one of the prime places to start a church, they discovered, was in Phoenix, Arizona, where Clark had grown up. This new plan would mean a whopping pay cut and an uncertain outcome. But, filled with faith, the Cotherns made their arrangements.

Like many Christians, Clark and Joy had long been committed to the practice of tithing: giving God 10 percent of their earnings each month, usually via the collection basket at church. It was not that God needed their money; it was simply necessary for them to acknowledge that God was first in every aspect of their lives, even the material, and that they were completely dependent upon him. Tithing was easy for them; they had enough money and were used to being generous with their belongings and their time, as well as their cash. "Each time we moved, instead of carting all our furniture to a new location, we always gave some of it away to people who had greater needs than we did," Clark explains. "It wasn't that we were so saintly—we just couldn't see the point of dragging stuff all over the country."

Now, preparing for Phoenix, they decided to give most of their furniture, including baby supplies, to an expectant couple in college. "Our two tots were still in diapers, but we felt that our family was complete, so others should get some use out of their clothes and equipment," Clark recalls. The college couple delightedly carted the huge load away. Only a few weeks later, Joy discovered she was expecting a third child.

The couple was excited, but the timing was tough on Joy. By the time they had loaded their gear and set off for Phoenix, she was in the throes of morning sickness. Somewhat belatedly, Clark was realizing that obedience to God's calls often costs the family as much or more than the one who is being called. But once in Phoenix, he was able to throw himself into his work—starting Bible-study groups, writing pamphlets, and calling on potential church members. Joy was left in a non-air-conditioned house, which sometimes reached 120 degrees during July, with two demanding toddlers, and a pervasive worry over how they were going to provide financially for the new baby.

Unpaid bills mounted, and no help came. As her little ones fussed and her back ached, Joy often wondered, *What are we doing in this desert?* Had they heard God's directions clearly? If so, where was the help they needed?

Clark struggled with his own inadequacies. Some folks seemed less than enthusiastic about this fledgling church than he had anticipated; would he get it off the ground? Would he make enough money to support Joy and the children? Was he doing this for God, or for his own ego satisfaction? He found no answers anywhere.

One morning, as the baby's due date neared, things came to a head. It was time for Clark to write the monthly tithe check to the church. For the first time, he balked. Tithing had made sense when they *had* money, but now . . . he threw his pen down on the table. Wasn't it a little ridiculous to give away some of their precious funds, then ask God to replenish the money so they could buy clothes and diapers? Why not just shortcut the process—keep the tithe money, and spend it on their newborn? It was logical, wasn't it? He turned to Joy. "I know that God always provides when we put him first. But I'm so tired of hand-me-downs. Maybe I should use this money to buy some things you need."

Joy nodded, dispiritedly. "Just once I'd like to have something new. And I'd like our baby to wear a nice outfit to the church's grand opening, instead of these stained hand-me-downs." She sighed, and, in her quiet way, made an enormous leap of faith. "But if you think we should give the money to the church, it's fine with me."

Silence fell. Would God take care of their needs if they didn't help him do it? Yet, if Clark didn't lead by example, how would those in his new congregation learn what trust in God really meant?

They looked at each other in wordless understanding. They had made a commitment, and they would stay the course, whether it made sense through earthly eyes, or not. Slowly, Clark picked up the pen, wrote the tithe check, then looked at the balance that remained. Just enough for milk and bread until payday.

The following morning, a United Parcel Service truck pulled up in front of their house. The driver wrestled a huge box to the door. "There must be some mistake," Joy told him as she looked at the box's return address. "We don't know anyone in North Carolina."

The driver shrugged. "Is your name Cothern?"

"Yes."

"Then it's for you."

Puzzled, Joy signed the receipt. Clark came up behind her and looked at the box. "We don't know anyone in North Carolina."

"True," said Joy. "But I guess someone there knows us."

Clark got scissors and opened the top. Just inside were snapshots, all of smiling strangers from a church congregation in North Carolina. Next to the pile of snapshots was a note. "We called your mission board. We asked for the name and address of a missionary family about to have a baby, and they sent us yours. We hope you enjoy opening these things as much as we enjoyed wrapping them. Know that God cares for you, and we do, too."

Joy started to cry. Because under the note were packages and packages and *more* packages, all wrapped in baby shower paper, and all containing items for their infant. God hadn't forgotten, after all. During the depths of their worry, he had already provided everything they would need.

Little Callie Elizabeth, born a few weeks later, was probably the prettiest girl at the church's successful grand opening. And amid all the excitement, the Cotherns pondered their miracle. Why had a North Carolina congregation felt led to supply strangers with a layette, instead of food or adult clothing or money? Surely there were other deserving mission families; why had the Cotherns been chosen? Perhaps most significant was the affirmation they had received, just when they needed it most: *Know that God cares for you, and we do, too.* How had it all come about?

They never found the answers. But through the years, as the children grew, Clark's ministry flourished and God provided many other examples of his love. The baby box became the symbol of it all. "Success isn't measured in dollars, but in how obedient we are to what we believe to be God's will," Clark says. "His purposes are often different from ours, because he's accomplishing things for eternity." When God's people step out in faith, they are blessed. Just ask the Cotherns.

MARVELOUS MICHAEL

Saint Michael the Archangel, defend us in battle . . .

—PRAYER TO ST. MICHAEL

Angels protect us physically, of course. But they also do battle for our souls. There are many negative forces in society, all competing for our attention, and the angels know only too well that, if left vulnerable, we can easily succumb. Take Jennifer Hughes* for example. "By training and previous career, I'm a research analyst," she says. "And while my work grounded me very well in the scientific method, it left my spiritual life in tatters. Although raised a Catholic, I was agnostic, basically atheist, for many years."

About three years ago, Jennifer became quite worried about a friend we'll call Charles. Charles was going through a painful time in his life. "His girlfriend left him suddenly, his business went under, and he discovered that his partner couldn't cosign for the debt," Jennifer explains. To make everything worse, Charles was also taking care of his infirm parents and trying to handle the stress such

*Name changed

a situation inevitably brings. (Charles, too, had been raised Catholic and had left the church years before.)

One evening, Jennifer went to a party. "In the kitchen there was a large artsy photo of a copper statue of an angel in an old grave-yard. The picture was very striking; the angle of the photo and the oxidation of the copper made the head almost look like a dreamlike skull, so it got my attention." Other guests were also struck by it.

"That's one tough-looking angel," remarked a man standing next to Jennifer.

"It's St. Michael the Archangel," the host pointed out. "A photographer friend gave it to us." Jennifer was strangely taken with the photo and decided to put her research skills to work to find out more about St. Michael.

Over the next two weeks, Jennifer literally tripped over references to Michael. "I found an ad for a small church named St. Michael the Archangel. I passed a mailbox with the name of M. Mons (a story I had read had St. Michael appearing at the battle of Mons during the First World War). Every other male I met, it seemed, was named Michael. Michael, Michael, everywhere." She had never even thought about him, and now she seemed to be deluged with mentions of his name. "I got an impulse to look up novenas on the Internet and see if there was one for the Archangel Michael."

A novena is simply a prayer that has a specific intention and is prayed nine days in a row. Jennifer had never said a novena before.

And of course, she no longer believed in prayer. "If scientists had to believe in prayer in order to test it, we'd never get there!" she says. "Instead, we start with tests, not beliefs. Many of us *want* to believe, but we're not sure *what* to believe." Despite her hesitation, when Jennifer did indeed find a novena to St. Michael, she was interested. It struck her as something good to say for someone in a time of trouble. She decided to say it for Charles, asking St. Michael particularly that Charles be guided through this painful time and that he rediscover his creativity and artistic ability, which he had allowed to fall into disuse.

Jennifer wasn't sure what else was needed. Not having been in church in years, and not very eager to visit one, she instead went to the grocery store to buy a candle that she could light when praying for Charles. It was a Saturday, and the store was crowded; however the checkout lane nearest the candle display was completely empty. "I went there," she says. "The clerk and the bagger were both young men. They were cheerful, quick, and continually cracking jokes. I looked at their nametags. Both were named Michael." And when she reached her car, she noticed that the vehicle parked next to her had a vanity license plate reading, E-TRNL.

Jennifer took these as positive signs and wrote them all down in her research journal. She also told Charles what she was planning, in case he had any objections. Charles simply thanked her. "I hope it works," he said.

Jennifer hoped so, too. Faithfully she said the prayer each day, although it was not what many would consider faith-filled prayer—more like "If you are out there, I am appreciative" with a plea attached. But what could it hurt? On the ninth and final day, after praying, she thought, *I really hope this works.* "As soon as that thought formed in my mind, I heard this firm voice in my head say emphatically: "Done!"

And it was. Today, Charles is far happier in his personal life, and he's doing creative work that he never would have been able to do had his original business succeeded. What turned out to be yet another sign is that Charles' birthday is September 29, which, in the Catholic tradition, is St. Michael's feast day.

"I have read religious writers who feel that prayers like mine show a lack of faith," Jennifer says. "But that's the point: if skeptics had faith, they would be believers, wouldn't they? God does not seem to be offended by skeptical prayers. God just shows up." Today, Jennifer leads a Bible-study group, and although she defines her faith life now as "full of experiments!" she also makes time for prayer and meditation. Heaven had to put a neon sign in front of her so she would start listening. But she's grateful each day to St. Michael for leading her back home.

A Man Called George

Good and bad acts have a "ripple" effect—they set off a chain reaction of consequences, both positive and negative. No act is an act in isolation.

—John Ronner

Ann McAllister Clark's father had died recently, and she was still feeling the loss of his presence. She felt a curious sorrow that surfaced at unexpected moments. In part, this was because she and her father—while loyal to one another—had never been close in the way good friends are close. Ann had been a lifelong lover of books, had majored in literature in college, and had recently opened a used bookstore in her small town of Middleville, Michigan. Mr. McAllister, by contrast, was a lawyer, apparently disinterested in all but the driest of writings.

But Ann's sense of loss deepened shortly after the funeral, when she found her father's college diplomas and realized with shock that he, too, had majored in literature at the University of Michigan. Why had he never told her, never alluded to a shared interest that might have bridged some of the gap between them? Ann felt cheated, almost embittered at the missed opportunity.

One day while boxing his law books, she found a fine 1909 set of Harvard Classics, each volume bearing his signature. "Very lightly, I ran my fingers over the inscriptions," Ann says. "Touching them somehow made me feel his presence." She discovered other excellent works, too, but the Harvard Classics were her favorites. Why hadn't he signed any of his other books? Ann would never know. But the Classics made him seem closer. She would keep this treasured collection always.

The family finished packing Mr. McAllister's belongings, and everyone took some keepsakes. They held a sale, then arranged an auction for the leftovers. "Not those," Ann cautioned the auctioneer's burly sons as she pointed to the boxes containing the Classics. "Just take the law books. The rest will go home with me." But three days after the auction, she discovered that the set of Harvard Classics was not in the boxes she had taken. Every volume, each with her father's signature, was gone.

Ann fought down panic. *You're a former antiques dealer,* she reminded herself sternly. *You know how to trace sales records. You'll find the books.* But it was no use. The Classics had apparently been sold quickly, then again, and yet again. Hopelessly gone. Probably gathering dust on someone's top shelf, halfway around the country. To her, the final link with her father was now forever broken.

Swallowing her sorrow, Ann returned to her new project, the used bookstore. There were few customers, and she worried about whether she could keep going. Yet the store brought her a small measure of comfort, and she needed that right now.

One quiet morning, an elderly man wandered in. He did not seem to be in the market for a used book. Ann noticed the perspiration on his forehead, the eyes slightly glazed. As a diabetic, Ann had occasionally recognized fellow sufferers; this man might be one. On the other hand, he might be mentally disturbed. Was she in danger, or was he? "Do you need help?" she asked.

"Why do you ask?" he responded, somewhat belligerently.

Should she call 911, and turn him over to others? No, she saw in him a vulnerability she could relate to. Surely she could reach out, just a little. "What can I do for you?" she asked again, gently, as if approaching a frightened deer.

"I'm George, and I've just gotten out of the hospital," the man explained. "I have high blood sugar—but I knew I was going to be sick before it happened. I see things that others cannot see."

Ann thought again about 911. Her visitor probably did have diabetes, but he was obviously delusional as well. "Do you have anyone at home to care for you?" she asked.

"My wife. But she's tired of all these things." George explained that, the day before, on the drive to the hospital, the road had been strewn with beautiful flowers—like a sign that all would be well.

But his wife couldn't see them. On another occasion, his deceased mother had appeared at the foot of his bed, holding a small lyre. She had handed it to George to play, and he had done so, although he had never played any musical instrument before. His wife had slept right through it. There were other examples, too, lots of them.

Ann wondered if George was running a high fever. People hallucinated during fevers, didn't they? "George," she put a hand on his arm, "You've just gotten out of the hospital, and your blood sugar is out of whack."

"So?"

"So, I care about you. Why don't you go home, have a light supper, take a warm bath, get into bed, and listen to some soothing music. Rest and sleep. Your body needs it."

"You don't believe me," George said. Then he smiled, and went out the front door. Ann smiled back. He had not taken offense, and that was good. But would he get home safely?

Ann worried about George all evening. Perhaps she should search for him, or tell someone about him. But that might cause more problems for him, instead of soothing the ones he already had. Maybe she shouldn't have gotten involved. Yet, wasn't that what life was supposed to be about, watching out for one another? Finally, she decided that if she didn't see George the following day, she would contact the police.

Shortly after she opened the store the next morning, however, George arrived. A rejuvenated George, with pink, healthy skin and smiling eyes. "George!" Ann exclaimed. "You look great!"

He explained that her concern had touched him, and he had gone home and done everything she suggested. "I don't think I have slept that well in months. And it was all because of you."

She protested a bit, saying that she hadn't done much, just what any fellow diabetic would do.

But George had more to say. "I came in here yesterday because I knew you were lonely and worried about business picking up." How had he known? Was it so obvious after all? "I wanted to help you," George was explaining, "and you ended up helping me instead. So I've brought you a present. Some books."

Just what Ann needed—more used books that no one would probably ever buy. She tried to look enthusiastic and grateful as George went out to his car and carried in two brown paper bags. It was enough that he seemed more normal today. She could always get rid of this latest batch after he left.

But when she pulled out the first few books, she saw that they were Harvard Classics. "George! I lost a set of my father's just like these!" George nodded, as if he knew all about it. Ann continued to unpack the books. Amazing. The covers were the same as the lost set, maroon leather.

Slowly she opened the first book. There was her father's signature.

It was impossible. Yet the set was complete, each volume bearing the familiar inscription. Her father's final gift, returned as a result of her own compassion. She touched the writing, then lifted tear-filled eyes to George. "How?"

But the question was too big, and George would only smile. "You see? I do know things."

George visited the store several times after delivering the treasured books. "I believe he was lonely and needed company," Ann says. "I just let him talk." But he never explained how he had gotten the books, and she never asked. Later, she sold the store to an employee, and now, along with a writing career, runs a rare books business on the Internet.

But whenever Ann becomes discouraged or lonely, she remembers the blessing of that moment of discovery, her father's unexpected message of love and connection, the awareness that what goes around truly comes around. And she touches the signature again.

RISKS THAT BROUGHT RESULTS

Prayer begins where human capacity ends.

—MARIAN ANDERSON

Zazel Whitney, of Woodland Hills, California, was concerned when her grown daughter Elizabeth* announced that she was taking a sightseeing trip, alone, to Yellowstone National Park. Driving through such wilderness would be a bit hazardous for anyone, but Elizabeth had been stricken with multiple sclerosis ten years before, and had gradually become too disabled to work or even walk. "She lives independently, drives a car with hand–controls, and brings her wheelchair wherever she goes," Zazel explains. "I try not to be overly protective, but I do worry about her." Although Elizabeth had camped outdoors many times, on this trip she was planning to stay

*not her real name

at a hotel. Despite this added protection, Zazel was still nervous. But she knew she couldn't dissuade her courageous daughter, so she began to pray for Elizabeth instead.

A day or two after Elizabeth had left on the trip, Zazel stopped at a gas station on her way home from work. A woman wearing a nurse's uniform, with a stethoscope sticking out of her pocket, approached Zazel as she filled her car's tank. The woman had apparently been crying.

"What's the matter?" Zazel looked up. "Are you in trouble?"

"Yes, I am," the nurse replied tearfully. "I had a flat tire on the freeway, and had no spare. A nice man stopped, and drove me here to buy a tire. But my car is old, and this station doesn't sell oversized tires." She wiped her eyes.

"What are you going to do?" Zazel asked.

"The man said he knew where he could pick up a used tire of that size for thirty dollars," the nurse said. "He left, and I went to the ATM station next door to get thirty dollars to repay him when he comes back. But I've lost my wallet with my card in it, and I have no cash." Tears filled her eyes again. "Could you . . . could you *possibly* lend me thirty dollars?"

Zazel thought for a moment. She didn't have any cash either. But she could write a check to this helpful man, and the nurse could reimburse her later—if she believed the nurse's story. Actually, she didn't. The whole situation seemed contrived—why would an anonymous passerby spend time buying a tire for someone he didn't know? And was it logical that this woman would lose her wallet just when she most needed it? Besides, Zazel had been raised to be leery of strangers.

But what if the story was true? What would Jesus do in such a situation? What would he have Zazel do? She often asked herself that question. And when the nurse kept weeping, Zazel decided to help.

The nurse had written the man's name on a piece of paper, so Zazel wrote a check for thirty dollars to him. Then the women exchanged addresses and phone numbers, and they sat in Zazel's car, waiting for the man to return with the tire. By now, the nurse had calmed down. "You are so sweet to help me," she said. "What would I have done without you?"

But Zazel wondered what the nurse would do if this man never reappeared. It was getting late, and Zazel had other chores to complete. Reluctantly, she left the woman at the gas station. "I'll mail you your money as soon as I get home," the nurse called after her. "Thanks again!"

During the next week, Zazel decided that, after she received the repayment in the mail, she would call the woman to find out how things had worked out. But a week passed, then another, and no payment arrived. Zazel felt foolish. Maybe there hadn't been a helpful man and a flat tire after all—maybe Zazel had simply been the victim of a clever scam. Why hadn't she been wise enough to spot it? She still had the phone number of the nurse's agency for whom the woman worked, if it wasn't a fake, too. "Should I call her and ask about the money?" Zazel asked her husband.

"Why? You did a good thing, and you're only out thirty dollars. Let it go."

Her husband was right. Only her pride had been injured. Jesus knew her motive, and his view was the one she needed to trust. She tossed the nurse's number away. And when the canceled check came back, endorsed with the name Zazel had inscribed, she filed it, too, without attempting to trace the man.

Zazel's daughter Elizabeth returned from her trip on a Saturday night, and Zazel met her at church the next morning. "How did everything go?" she asked, relieved to see her daughter in one piece.

"Oh Mom, it was great, but you'll never guess what happened! I had a flat tire in the wilds of Utah on the way home." Since she couldn't walk, she held up her sun visor that said NEED HELP, CALL POLICE.

"A nice person stopped and changed my tire, so I drove to a roadside park to have my lunch," Elizabeth went on. "Another tourist sat down next to me, and when I told her what happened, she reminded me that my spare was just for short trips—I couldn't get all the way to Los Angeles on it. But what was I supposed to do now?

How could I find a tire big enough for my car, especially in such a remote area? Plus I didn't have any cash left, just a credit card."

Zazel was starting to get goosebumps. The story sounded familiar.

"The tourist volunteered to get me a secondhand tire that was the right size," Elizabeth went on. "It took a lot of trust for me to wait there in the park, all by myself. What if it got dark and she didn't return?"

"But did she?"

"Yes, with the tire. But when I asked for her address so I could send her the money for it, she said, 'Oh, we're church people—we do things like this for others all the time.' She wouldn't let me reimburse her, Mom. Can you believe it?"

Zazel could. And suddenly, she saw her own situation through spiritual eyes. Maybe she had not been the victim of a clever con artist, after all. Perhaps she had been given a chance to sow something another could reap, to send ahead a blessing that her own daughter would soon need. Did such things happen? How would she ever know?

In Bonnie's case, the outcome was different. "Every morning when I got off the commuter train, I'd pass this homeless man on my way to work," she relates. "I have never gotten involved with people like this because I have mixed feelings—would my donation buy drugs for them, or enable them to stay helpless?" Yet, Bonnie seemed drawn to this particular man. Like Zazel, she found herself asking a different question: what would Jesus have her do?

Gradually, Bonnie made eye contact with this man. Brief conversations followed. His name was Phil, he told her, and he had been on the streets about a year. Beyond that, he would not elaborate. Sometimes Bonnie's only connection with Phil was a smile and a cheery greeting. At other times, she'd bring him a sandwich or give him some coins. "The people at my office teased me unmercifully," she says. "They felt I was a soft touch and hopelessly gullible." But she kept on; somehow it just seemed right.

One day, however, Phil was not at his usual post. Weeks passed, and he didn't return. Bonnie was concerned, but the merchants and police officers along her route didn't know what had happened to him. Gradually, she forgot about Phil.

But one morning, when she passed the corner, someone called her name. She turned around. Coming toward her was Phil! But not the same disheveled beggar she had befriended over a year ago. No, this Phil was clean-shaven, clear-eyed, wearing a suit and a smile. "Phil! What happened to you?"

"*You* did, Bonnie." He was standing in front of her now, and she could hardly believe the change in him.

"Me? I didn't—"

"Oh, but you did. You, and two men who work together on the next block. For that whole year I lived on the streets, you three were the only ones who saw me as a *person*. You looked at me and talked to me. One day I asked myself: if there are three people in the world who believe in me, why can't I believe in me? So I went into rehab, and here I am."

He had a new job and wouldn't be downtown anymore. So he had come to his old corner one last time, to see if he could locate the three who had changed his life. "I found the men yesterday," he said. "I was just waiting for you."

"Whatever you did for one of these least brothers of mine, you did for me" (Matthew 25:40). Bonnie could hardly see Phil through the tears in her eyes. But she knew now the source of that unusual urge to get involved, if only in a small way. How glad she was that she had obeyed![2]

A woman named Jacqueline posted a similar experience on a Web site. In the mid-eighties, she owned a holistic health center on Martha's Vineyard near a center for the elderly. Jacqueline realized how little pampering such people received, so she and her assistant decided to donate their services to the center every Friday. "We massaged shoulders and gave foot rubs to anyone who wanted one," Jacqueline says, "and we also talked with the people, asking them questions and appreciating their wisdom."

Eventually, Jacqueline had to drop the service. She had saved up a little money toward a home of her own, and when a real estate agent told her about a few acres that would be going on the market soon, Jacqueline went to look at the land. "It was just what I'd been hoping to find," she says, "but I knew that, even scrimping, I could only come up with about half the selling price." For some reason, however, she asked the agent to write up an offer on those terms.

The agent was reluctant. "It's rude to put in such a low offer," she told Jacqueline. "You know it will never be accepted."

"This isn't a negotiation tactic," Jacqueline assured her. "It's honestly all I can afford." The agent wrote up the offer, shaking her head. The following day, Jacqueline's offer was accepted. Both women were astonished, because the land was definitely worth the asking price.

A few weeks later, Jacqueline met the seller. "I suppose you're wondering why I let the land go at a reduced price," she said.

"I certainly am."

The woman smiled. "This land is my mother's, and I'm selling it for her. She's one of the women whose feet you used to rub at the senior center." Jacqueline's mouth dropped open. "My mother told me many times how much she appreciated those massages, and how much better she felt afterwards," the woman continued. "I was happy to do something for you in return."

"I never knew, way back then, that these little acts of kindness would come back years later," says Jacqueline, "and end up saving me a small fortune in return." She calls it a mini-miracle—and why not?

Zazel Whitney didn't get to see the end of her story—and may never know the "why" of it. Bonnie and Jacqueline were more fortunate. But often, we aren't meant to control or even understand results. It's enough that God has asked, "Will you do this for me?" and we have answered, "Yes."

HOLY FRUITS OF FRIENDSHIP

Make friends with the angels, who though invisible are always with you.
Often invoke them, constantly praise them, and make good use of their
help and assistance in all your temporal and spiritual affairs.

—St. Francis de Sales

Ron Johnson was delighted. He had just paid off the mortgage on his duplex in Salt Lake City. Now he no longer needed the rental income from the second unit, so he could follow a long-held dream: remodeling the building into one wonderful house.

Ron hadn't contracted for any of the work yet when he discovered that Joe, one of his friends, needed an apartment. "I had met Joe when I was teaching country dancing," Ron recalls. "He was a quick learner and really enjoyed himself. People liked him a lot."

Ron decided that the duplex remodeling could wait, and he offered to rent the vacant apartment to Joe. Joe gratefully accepted.

Landlord and tenant got along well. "Joe was an auto mechanic with an amazing ability to use common sense to figure things out," Ron says. He knew Joe had been divorced some years back and had two children and several siblings. His family ties seemed loose— when Joe hosted a party to celebrate his parents' fiftieth wedding anniversary, for example, some of his brothers and sisters didn't attend. Nor did Joe's children visit very often. Joe didn't talk much about his family situation, however, and Ron respected his privacy.

Besides, he was busy enough with his sign business, located next door to his duplex, as well as involvement in several community organizations. And when Christmas rolled around each year, Ron was a self-described "yuletide lunatic," displaying trimmed trees, a nativity scene, a holiday village, and many other decorations both inside and out. "Mine is one of those houses that stops traffic and is always on the newspaper's list of 'places to see.'" That Christmas, Joe got into the spirit, too, building several animated characters and, with Ron, a marvelous miniature carousel.

"You know," he told Ron one night, "you've rekindled my love of this season. I guess I'd lost the meaning of it all during some difficult times. But it's back."

Joe had lived in the duplex for just over a year when he suffered a seizure and was subsequently diagnosed with a terminal illness.

It was a tremendous blow. "Yet Joe was determined to fight and not let anything ruin whatever time he had left," Ron says. Soon, environmental conditions at the garage where Joe worked aggravated his illness, and he had to quit his job. His income dropped drastically, and he could no longer afford to rent Ron's apartment.

"You've been planning to remodel it anyway," Joe told Ron one evening. "If I move out, you can start the work now."

"But where would you go?" Ron was still shocked at this turn of events. He knew that, thus far, none of Joe's relatives had offered help.

Joe shrugged. Did his living arrangements really matter at this point?

To Ron, they did. "You'll stay in the apartment, rent free," he said. Joe began to protest, but Ron insisted. "Rent free. And I don't want to hear another word about it."

Joe agreed, on the condition that Ron would allow him to start the planned renovations. When Ron said that the work would be too demanding, Joe assured him that it would not. "Besides," he pointed out, "it's a way that I can give something back to you, to thank you." Ron relented.

Joe started treatment, and the men began remodeling. Over the next months, as Joe delightedly showed interested visitors the changes he was making on the house, his health improved. In November, when Joe performed in a country dancing show at the

University of Utah, and later put up Ron's huge outdoor Christmas display, his illness seemed almost a thing of the past. But in January, doctors discovered a brain tumor. Joe's time was running out.

Ron refused to put Joe in a nursing home for his final days, despite paralysis on his right side and other difficult symptoms. Instead, Ron rented a hospital bed for his house, and he alerted Joe's friends. With their help, and visits from hospice nurses and Joe's two children, Joe stayed in the house where he had so enjoyed life. "A few of Joe's relatives came to see him during the last week or so," Ron says. "For some, it was the first time. But when Joe died, a friend and I were the only ones with him. Sally was holding his left hand, and I his right. At the moment of death, I became aware of a movement up the wall near his head, as if his spirit was leaving his body. Then, with his paralyzed hand, he squeezed mine in a firm grip." An involuntary motion? Perhaps. But Sally, holding Joe's good hand, felt nothing at all. "I thought then, and still do," says Ron, "that it was his way of thanking me for my help, and letting me know that everything on the other side was okay."

Because Joe's financial situation had been precarious, he had prepaid some of his final expenses, but not enough. And although his relatives had assured Ron that they would cover any additional costs, no one actually volunteered when the money was finally needed. So Ron arranged the funeral and signed papers making him legally responsible for the remaining charges. It was, he felt, his last act of commitment. He had forfeited rent money and would spend more at the mortuary—and maybe some folks thought he was a fool. But hadn't Jesus pointed out that the greatest of all loves was to lay down one's life (and presumably one's material goods) for a friend?

Word about Ron's generosity got around, and checks from Joe's friends started coming in to the funeral home. By the time Ron received the final bill, it had been cut to $1393. Still a sacrifice for him, but Ron paid it promptly, and closed a chapter in his life. Or so he assumed.

One evening the following summer, Ron was working in his garden. As he finished putting food on the last plant, he heard a command in his mind: "Take the fertilizer bag to the garage."

Ron paused. Why would he do that? He always stored fertilizer off the patio, much closer to the garden. Again, he heard the voice: "Take the bag to the garage." Ron obeyed.

At the same moment, a friend of Ron's who had stopped by came up the basement stairs. He, too, heard a voice: "You dropped your checkbook. Go back for it." Instantly, the friend turned and went down the stairs.

Just then, a gust of wind broke a huge limb from a tree behind the garage and sent it crashing across the patio and through the open basement door, right where the men had been. They stared in astonishment. "Only later did the shakes hit," Ron says. "I realized that if we hadn't heeded those warnings, we surely would have been killed."

Despite carrying homeowner's insurance for twenty-two years, Ron had never had a claim, and didn't know if such damage would be covered. He called the company, and a representative came out. "The tree needs to be cut up," Ron explained. "And the wall replaced, and the hole in the deck patched." The adjuster nodded and left.

Weeks passed, and Ron heard nothing from the company. Unfamiliar with the procedure, Ron assumed the claim had been denied, so he decided to hire people to do the work. His brother, however, had a chain saw. "We can cut those limbs ourselves," he told Ron. They did. Once they hauled the mess away, Ron realized that, although he rarely kept such products on hand, he had just enough of the perfect patching material to fix the hole himself rather than hire a professional. And instead of replacing the damaged wall, he tore it out. It was backbreaking, time-consuming work, but the new area looked even better than it had before.

Shortly after the repairs were done, Ron received a letter from the insurance company. There was no itemized bill included to show just how the company had arrived at its total, just an explanation that the enclosed check should reimburse him for his property damages. They hadn't denied the claim after all! Pleased, Ron looked at the check, and a chill ran through him. It was made out for $1393, the exact amount he had spent on Joe's funeral four months before.

The memories came to him: Joe homeless, ill, lonely, Ron doing his best to help because he could imagine no other course. Now, with utter certainty, he knew. This check, this entire rescue in the yard, wasn't a coincidence at all. While he had been watching out for his friend, God had been watching out for him.

"I've never been real religious, but I've always believed there was 'something else,'" Ron says today. "Now I believe that we're all here for a specific reason. We have lessons to learn and things we need to teach others by our example. There is much more to life than the reality we see around us."

PART 4

JUST FOR THE HOLIDAYS

Wonder at Wal-Mart

More things are wrought by prayer
Than this world dreams of.
—"Morte d'Arthur," Alfred, Lord Tennyson

On Thanksgiving weekend, in Ruby Lee Whitehurst's town of Williamston, North Carolina, the local Wal-Mart holds the biggest sale of the season. Ruby wouldn't dream of missing any Thanksgiving sale, but this year she had decided to stretch her budget as far as it could go. Ruby is the community educator for a local domestic violence/sexual assault organization, and she spends much of her workday conducting presentations and workshops about these topics. Needless to say, the work can be grim, but Ruby loves people, and she puts her heart into it. And this year, she wanted to do even more.

For example, her twenty-four-year-old son Kevin needed a new coat. "He lives alone, but finances are sometimes strained, and he wouldn't buy himself much that's new." There were Ruby's two dogs, who, of course, were members of the family. Ruby's sister is a single mom with three children, so Ruby would, as always, provide some treats for their Christmas stockings. "I also work with a young and wonderful single mother who I will call Jessie," Ruby says. "Jessie is from Puerto Rico, and she has two little boys and a two-year-old daughter, Brianna. She struggles to pay bills and buy the kids the necessities of life, and since we get paid only once a month, it's not easy." As Thanksgiving approached, Jessie was becoming anxious.

For this reason, Ruby had decided to add gifts for each of Jessie's children to her already long list. She had mentioned this to Jessie and asked for suggestions. Jessie was dumbfounded and delighted. Shyly, she said that little Brianna longed for a Cabbage Patch doll, and the boys wanted remote-control cars. So on Thanksgiving Friday, Ruby got to Wal-Mart early to start her search. Such traditional favorites shouldn't be hard to find.

The store was crowded already, but Ruby didn't see any Cabbage Patch dolls or remote-control cars. After searching for a while, she reluctantly gave up and purchased some other items for Jessie's children. They would be grateful for anything.

Once at home, however, Ruby began to feel restless. "My spirit was telling me to purchase the Cabbage Patch baby and two remote-control cars, as I had originally planned. So off to Wal-Mart I went, for the second time that day. As soon as I walked through the door, I saw a stack of very nice Dodge Ram remote-control cars. They hadn't been there earlier, but what luck that now they were right in the front of the store! I scooped up a red one and a black one."

Now for the doll. There was a shelf just ahead of her with a few Cabbage Patch babies on it. But Ruby wanted a Hispanic doll. "I wanted Brianna to have a doll with brown skin and eyes, looking just like her."

There was one doll that seemed close, and finally Ruby put it in her cart. But it just wasn't right. Ruby realized that an older woman had passed her several times, noticing her dilemma. However, she didn't seem to be one of the Wal-Mart staff, just a shopper, like Ruby. Now the woman approached. "There's another shelf of Cabbage Patch dolls, high up against the wall, at the back of the store," she suggested. "Maybe you'll find what you're looking for there."

"Oh! Thank you." Ruby turned toward the back of the store. What an odd place to put more dolls. As she approached the wall, the same woman appeared ahead of her, turned, smiled, and pointed to the display. Again Ruby thanked her.

The display was certainly high, and the babies all looked the same, except for one. Ruby asked a young man to get a particular doll down for her. "They're all the same," he protested. "Just like the one in your cart."

Ruby refused to back down. "I'd like *that* one." She pointed again. Shrugging, the young man climbed up, retrieved the box, and passed the doll into Ruby's outstretched hands. Brown skin, brown eyes . . . Ruby looked at the doll's "birth certificate" and gasped. "Consuelo Tavia" was the doll's name—an Hispanic baby for an Hispanic child. And the only Hispanic doll there.

"I was thrilled all the way home, just thinking about it," Ruby says. "The next day, Thanksgiving Saturday, I went back to Wal-Mart to get a few more gifts on my list."

Perhaps she would buy another remote-control car for her nephew. But when she entered the store, the display was nowhere to be seen. Could they have sold the entire bin in one day? Not likely. The cars must be somewhere else.

Ruby looked up and down the aisles, but she was not able to locate the cars. "I'm sorry—I don't recall any bin with cars in it," more than one clerk told her. Ruby had reached the back of the store when she realized something else. Although she was standing in the exact spot as yesterday, there was no wall display of Cabbage Patch babies there, nor did the wall look as if there had ever been anything on it.

Jessie and her children were ecstatic over the presents. And Ruby? She doesn't wonder why heaven would be concerned over a special gift for a little child. "I think the angels take very good care of us," she says. "Nothing is too small for God."

With Songs of Rejoicing

Jesus is the reason for the season.

—HOLIDAY SLOGAN

She should never have waited so long to tackle the Christmas shopping, Kimberley Little reminded herself as she shifted her bundles from one aching arm to the other. She hated shopping, hated having to brave the crowds and sift through endless piles of merchandise. But there was only so much holiday gift buying one could do through catalogs, and, of course, the children needed their annual photo taken with Santa Claus. So here she was, imprisoned in a slow-moving "Visit Santa" line, wondering if she might spend the entire holidays in this Albuquerque mall.

Of course, she had to admit she was never "up" at this time of year, no matter how smoothly things went. Her father had died tragically in a plane crash just a few days before Christmas when Kimberley was fourteen, and although many years had passed, she never faced December without feeling echoes of that familiar shock, sorrow, and loneliness. As her faith matured, Kimberley had gotten involved in her church, singing in the choir and teaching her young sons to pray. She didn't doubt that her father was in heaven with Jesus, and she would see him again. But every year as Christmas approached, the same nagging question emerged: "This is all supposed to be so wonderful. So why isn't it?"

Kimberley shifted packages again, and looked at her three young sons. Their moods seemed no cheerier than hers. One was demanding a ride on the train further down the mall. Another was hungry. "I hate Christmas!" muttered the eldest, his lip thrust out in frustration.

Kimberley felt guilty. "Moms have so much influence on the spirit of the family," she says. "If we're just a little bit cranky, everyone picks up on it." She didn't want to spoil this season for the children. They shouldn't carry the same vague sadness that she did.

She glanced around at the other families in line. She realized that they were all like hers: the kids were irritable, tired, and fighting with one another; their parents were grimly Determined to Endure.

Why are we like this? Kimberley wondered. Where was the real Christmas, the spirit of love and peace, the angels rejoicing at a Savior's entrance into the world? How did a person cut through the confusion, the fatigue, the pressure—yes, even the sorrowful memories—to find it?

Suddenly, God nudged her. "It couldn't have been anything else," Kimberley says, "because all at once I felt a little tingle, as if something new was happening. And I realized that if I wanted to feel better about myself, I had to take the first step. I had to be brave." But how?

Sing a carol. The suggestion was already in her heart. She had recently performed a solo in church. She knew how to sing.

But this noisy shopping center was not church. "Oh, no, God, not me," she answered silently. "You remember how shy I am. People will stare."

Bring Christmas to the mall. Sing.

Kimberley sighed. It was no use. She knew that Voice. And hadn't she just asked God where Christmas was?

Softly she began to sing. "Silent night, holy night . . " The couple in front of her, who had been filling out a photography order form, paused and turned around.

"All is calm, all is bright." Kimberley reached for her youngest son and picked him up. What if they threw her out of the mall, for disturbing the peace?

You're bringing the peace, the answer came. *Sing.*

The children behind her had stopped arguing. "Listen," one whispered to the other. "That lady's singing."

The tips of Kimberley's ears turned red. "Round yon virgin, mother and child," she went on. Her sons would never speak to her again.

Was it her imagination, or did she hear another voice? And another? Yes, the couple in front of her was singing, their order form forgotten. Now the children behind her, and their parents, and the family next to them. Dazed, Kimberley realized that the entire section of the Santa Claus line had joined her. Even her own offspring.

It was true! Little risks could lead to wonderful things. And she *was* feeling better, her spirit soothed, her mind quieted. Maybe Christmas, and its eternal message, was simply as close as anyone allowed it to be.

Voices faded as the song ended. "Let's do 'Angels We Have Heard on High'" Kimberley suggested to the people around her. It was her eldest's favorite carol, and her dad had always liked it too.

It was going to be a wonderful Christmas.

Upon a Midnight Clear

And so, as Tiny Tim observed, God bless Us, Every One!
—Charles Dickens, *A Christmas Carol*

It was going to be a lean Christmas, Barbara and Ray Thill realized as they surveyed their budget early one December several years ago. Unexpected medical bills, major repairs on their house in Berwyn, Illinois, and the ongoing needs of a family of nine young children had left nothing extra for gifts under the tree.

There were other alternatives, of course. They could take out a loan or run up their credit cards. But the thought was unpalatable; they tried to be good stewards of their resources, and they were certain that unnecessary debt was not in God's plan for them.

Ray could look for a part-time job at night. "But I felt that the kids and I needed Ray's presence and help each evening more than the material things his extra paycheck could provide," Barbara explains.

Both also knew that if they mentioned their financial difficulties to friends or family, someone would find a way to help. However,

Barbara and Ray were used to giving help, not getting it, and they discounted this idea, too. They would say nothing to anyone and care for their family as best they could. Since all the children needed pajamas, they would buy those, maybe one or two little games to share, and some candy. They hoped the kids would understand.

The next day, Advent began, and Barbara explained the situation. "Just remember," she told the children gently, "we have a lot more than baby Jesus did. We have a warm house, good food, enough clothes, and lots of friends. The holy family had none of those things in Bethlehem. So this Christmas, just to show Jesus how grateful we are, let's give instead of receive." Her brother, a father of four youngsters, had been out of work for many weeks, and it would be a rough holiday for his family, too. "Why don't each of you choose one of your toys and wrap it up for Uncle Dick's children?" she suggested. "Otherwise, they won't have any celebration at all. And remember 'bread upon the waters.' What we give now, we'll receive a hundredfold in heaven."

The children were quiet for a moment, then one of the boys spoke up. "That's okay, Mom. Christmas is about Jesus' birthday, anyway." The others nodded, trying to look convinced.

Even the oldest, eleven-year-old Ray Jr.—who had longed for a big red sled for the past three Christmases—hid his disappointment. "I'll buy some stuff for our cousins from my paper route money," he told his mother.

She hugged each child, her beloved ones, her treasures. But her heart ached. What is worse than wanting to make someone you love happy and not being able to do it? Should she pray for extra money? No. Although it would not be inappropriate to do so, she believed that God had not forgotten them. And if he didn't want her and Ray to provide toys, he would have a good reason. Faith was a decision. And they had decided to leave Christmas in God's hands.

Advent continued. The older children attended Mass almost every morning on their way to school, and they helped the younger ones wrap a few secondhand toys for Uncle Dick's family. At night, around the dinner table, they told one another about the good things in their lives. "Blessings are presents, too," Barbara reminded them. "God doesn't wrap them in holiday paper, but they come from him just the same."

Christmas Eve finally arrived, and it was almost 10:00 p.m. before all the children were asleep. Barbara and Ray laid nine pajama-filled packages under the tree, stuffed nine stockings with candy, and smiled at each other. Their family was together, safe, and well, and there was even a little pile of gifts for Uncle Dick's children when the family came over tomorrow to share a big roasted turkey—and baby Jesus' birthday cake. Despite their hardships, joy was in the air. Christmas was almost here!

Down the street from the Thills lived Tom and Pat Daly and their family. Tom was not well acquainted with the Thills. He knew the family was large, but he would have been hard-pressed to identify anyone in it. Yet during Advent, when his wife heard a rumor that the Thills were going through a hard time, Tom began thinking about them.

What kind of a holiday would they have? Should he inquire? Would it embarrass them? After all, he was virtually a stranger, and they hadn't asked for help from neighbors who knew them far better than he did. What business was it of his, anyway?

Tom put the matter out of his mind. But it continued to nag at him. On December 23, he remembered something. "Say," he asked a teenage boy who had been working for him, "didn't you tell me awhile back that your dad was a toy salesman?"

"He's a jobber," the boy answered. "He calls on stores, shows them toy samples, and takes orders."

"What does he do with those samples when Christmas is over?" Tom was getting an idea. People could be angels, too, couldn't they?

The boy shrugged. "I dunno. But here's his phone number if you want to find out."

What would he say? Tom wasn't even sure what he wanted to ask. But on Christmas Eve morning, he contacted the jobber, who told him to stop by his warehouse. "When I got there, he took me to a room where there were several large toys, some in beat-up cartons," Tom says. "He waved his arm and told me to take whatever I needed."

Tom could hardly believe it! Whatever he needed! But what did he need? He didn't know how many Thill children there were, or their ages or genders. And since his car was quite small, space was going to be limited. What if he chose the wrong things?

Then Tom felt himself relaxing. This whole situation hadn't come about by accident; he was sure of that now. And the same One who arranged it would surely guide him in his selection. Tom looked at the toys. If he were a kid, which ones would *he* like? He took out one of the green plastic bags he'd brought along, and got started.

Barbara and Ray were just getting ready to go to bed when the phone rang. Who could be calling this late on Christmas Eve? Ray answered, spoke briefly, and hung up with a puzzled look. "It was Tom Daly—he lives down the street," he told Barbara.

"Yes, I've met his wife."

"Tom said that he just dropped off a few green bags out in front, some beat-up toy samples for the kids, if we can use them."

If they could use them! Barbara looked outside. There were the bags, lined up on the steps. Ray carried them in. And as she opened them, Barbara's eyes filled with tears.

The toys were beautiful, exquisite, far nicer than anything they'd have been able to afford, even in an affluent year. Even more astounding, there was one perfectly suited toy for each of the children. There were three dolls for the three girls, a baby toy for the baby, a fire engine almost as large as Larry and—Barbara blinked in amazement—a big red sled, just what Ray Jr. had always wanted. Thirteen toys in all. Nine for her brood and, incredibly, four extras for her brother's four children. No one had known about their need, or her brother's. Yet, someone had gone shopping just for them.

The next morning the children raced downstairs and shouted in wonder at the bounty in the living room. "Mom! You were only kidding about us not getting presents!" six-year-old Eddie shouted in delight.

"No, I wasn't . . ." Barbara tried to explain.

But Ray Jr. had the best answer. "It's 'bread upon the waters,'" he remarked thoughtfully. "We gave to God, and he gave it back, a hundredfold."

Years later, the Thill family still wonders about the event. There were more lean Christmases, of course, and additional family trials. But the joy of that morning sustained them through much, and it is still one of their most cherished memories. They think that, perhaps the Christmas blessing was not really the unexpected toys, but the continued reassurance that God is always with us. No matter how difficult life becomes, we have only to believe—and God will do the rest.[3]

Any Caring Person

Hate can make a lot of noise. Love and courage are usually quieter.
But in the end, they're the strongest.
—Janice Cohn, *The Christmas Menorahs: How a Town Fought Hate*

During the wee hours of Sunday morning, December 8, 1996, after the third night of Hanukkah, someone took a baseball bat and broke the front window of a house in Newtown, Pennsylvania. It might have been considered simple vandalism by the local police except for one significant factor: this house was the only one on the street with a lighted menorah in the window. The perpetrator had deliberately reached through the shattered window, took the menorah, and smashed it on the ground, breaking all eight bulbs.

The menorah is a symbol of the eight-day Jewish Festival of Lights, also known as Hanukkah, which occurs around the same time as Christmas. As a Nativity scene reminds Christians of their heritage and faith, a menorah does so for Jews. It is the symbol of a miracle that occurred for their ancestors centuries ago.

The woman who lives in the house in Newtown did not think of miracles when she found the shattered mess in her front yard. It was not the first time she and her family had been targeted. As a child, she had come with her mother (a Holocaust survivor) and father to the United States to escape persecution in the former Soviet Union. But now, as she viewed the smashed candelabra, the familiar fear returned.

Lisa Keeling, a young mother, lived down the street and heard about the incident when she and her family returned from Mass. "A neighbor left a message on my answering machine," Lisa says. "Because I am a former military police officer, he thought I might know the home phone number of our police chief so he could report this right away."

Lisa was appalled. Newtown is a pleasant town, which includes many cultures and religions Although there was occasional crime, she had never heard of anyone being singled out because of his or her faith or ethnicity. What effect would this have on the other Jewish families in the neighborhood? Would they be intimidated into turning off their menorahs? How would she feel if someone desecrated a statue of baby Jesus on her lawn? Unless everyone was free to practice religious beliefs, no one was.

Lisa was getting an idea. "I'd like to buy a menorah and put it in our front window, so that family will know they're not going through this alone," she told her husband. "If the vandals come back, they'll have us to target, too. What do you think?"

Lisa's husband could have pointed out that they had children, and could be vulnerable to retaliation. Instead, he didn't hesitate. "Go for it," he said.

Lisa returned her neighbor's call and told him about her idea. "Why don't you contact Margie Alexander?" he suggested. "She's doing the same thing."

Margie lived around the corner and was involved in the Neighborhood Watch program. She had been as horrified as Lisa when she heard the news.

"I work with women in health situations, so I know what pain can look like," Margie says. "When I went to see the woman whose menorah had been smashed, I saw that same pain on her face. I can't do much about the suffering I see at work, but I thought I could do something here." Margie was now driving from store to store looking for menorahs. "But they're almost impossible to find by now," she told Lisa over her cell phone.

Lisa began calling stores from home, then relaying locations where the candelabras were available to Margie. "Buy as many as you can," she said, since several Christian neighbors had dropped by, asking for instructions on where to purchase and how to display a menorah. Word was getting around.

Sundown—the time for lighting—had almost arrived by the time Margie sped home and distributed all that she had located. "I took down the Christmas lights in one of my windows and put the menorah there, all by itself," Lisa recalls. "I didn't want there to be any doubt about the statement we were making." Was she prepared for trouble? "Maybe," she says. "It passes through your mind. But it's just something you do."

That night when the Jewish woman turned onto her street, she stopped in amazement. Greeting her was a sea of lights, shining in silent solidarity, from the windows of all eighteen Christian households on her block, as if angels had taken up residence there. *We are with you* the warm glow seemed to say. Blinking back tears, she went home, replaced the broken bulbs in her own menorah, and put it back up in her window.

The vandals did not damage any property that night. Eventually, police arrested three teenage boys, who admitted that the neighborhood's unexpected show of strength and unity had deterred them from further activity. But they were not the only people affected. As the days of Hanukkah went on, Christian families from nearby blocks began to display menorahs alongside their wreaths and Nativity scenes. "I'd drive past and see a menorah in someone's window and think: *wait—I see that family at church—they're not Jewish.* Then it would dawn on me that they were supporting us as we supported the people on my block," Lisa recalls. Other Jewish families in the neighborhood, their confidence rising, turned their menorahs back on, too. Word spread as newspaper reporters and radio talk shows— even one in Israel—contacted the women for interviews. Pastors of local churches discussed the community response in their homilies, and a synagogue invited Lisa and Margie to a service so the congregation could thank them personally. "The rabbi gave us a book about something similar that had happened in Billings, Montana, in 1993," Lisa says. "Because of hate crimes there, the newspaper had printed the picture of a menorah on its front page, and thousands of people had hung the image in their windows. We had never heard about it, yet we ended up doing the same thing."[4]

Margie and Lisa are still amazed at all the attention they received because of what to them seems "something any caring person would do." But they now hang menorahs every year. "It's become a cherished part of my Christmas," Margie says, "because it represents a wonderful lesson I've learned: Just one little step in the right direction can have a domino effect. It can make life better for everyone."

HEAVEN ON THE HIGHWAY

Vision is the art of seeing things invisible.
—JONATHAN SWIFT, THOUGHTS ON VARIOUS SUBJECTS

It was Christmas week in Cleland, England, and Sharon Stead and her family had been visiting relatives. "Since our three sons were little—ages seven, five, and five months—we had planned to leave for home much earlier," Sharon recalls. But time had passed too quickly, and now they were facing a long drive on a single-lane road through miles of open country with few houses, services, or restaurants. Nor did the Steads own a cell phone. They had made the trip many times, but never this late in the day. Sharon was nervous, but she put on a smile as the families waved good-bye to one another. All too soon, darkness began to fall.

Snuggled up in warm fleecy blankets in the backseat, the boys went to sleep. But the road got darker, the terrain even more desolate. "Oh no," Sharon's husband, Dave, murmured about an hour into the journey. "Is that fog?"

It was. The dense fog floated over them, and soon they could barely see more than a few yards ahead. "As Dave braked, we both noticed the oil warning light flashing on and off on the dashboard. Then the engine began to sputter." The car seemed to lose power, chugging and bouncing along. The couple exchanged worried looks. There were no other cars in view, no sign of life anywhere. What if they stalled? How could they protect the children or find help?

There was nothing else to do but to pray. "God, please get us home safely," Sharon began. "Get the car home before it breaks down completely." Dave echoed her plea. Over and over the couple prayed as they watched the oil light flash on and off. The car continued to chug, slowing to about fifteen miles an hour. If they stopped, they might never get started again. Baby Lewis awakened and began to fuss. Somehow, Sharon got him into the front seat to give him his bottle. "I was afraid to stop praying, almost afraid to take my eyes off the dashboard light," she says. No cars appeared anywhere around them. Mile by mile, Dave continued to drive.

At last! Suddenly they saw lights ahead! It was an oasis, with a gas station right beside it. Gratefully, they pulled in just as the engine sputtered to a stop. They had made it! Or at least they were not alone anymore, for an attendant came toward them, smiling in welcome.

However, the news was not good. There were no mechanics on duty, nor was the oasis restaurant open. "The holidays, you know," the attendant pointed out. "It might take hours to find a mechanic. I can replace the oil you've lost, but I don't think that will get you home."

Dave didn't either. But there was no motel available, his family was cold and frightened, and he had to try. He and the mechanic replaced the oil, Dave got back in the car, and the engine started. Shakily they pulled out onto the lonely road. "Are we going to make it?" Sharon asked anxiously.

"Keep praying," Dave answered.

Sharon did, and somehow they kept moving. Even when they came upon an occasional stoplight, it was green, and they were able to coast through it without using the brake. Long after the oil should have run out, they finally reached the outskirts of their town, and at 2:30 a.m. they turned into their own driveway. It had taken them seven hours to cover a journey that usually took about four, but they were safe. Suddenly the car simply stopped running. Sharon and Dave prayed a loud "thank you!" before awakening the children.

"We truly believed that God had sent us the help we needed, and we were very grateful," Sharon says. But they did not realize how blessed they actually were until the next time they drove the same road back to their relatives' home in Cleland. For they passed no oasis or gas station on that journey. Nor have they ever seen such a place during the many years they have since driven the route. "We often tell the story of how God sent us a gas-station angel," Sharon says, "and a certain brand of blessed Christmas oil to bring us safely home."

OVER THE HILLS AND EVERYWHERE

The people who walked in darkness
have seen a great light;
Upon those who dwelt in the land of gloom
a light has shone.

—ISAIAH 9:1

Bud and Jane Surber of Salida, Colorado, are a remarkable couple. They've raised seven children and taken in sixty foster children, and now they enjoy frequent visits from twenty-one grandchildren, all on their large ranch, which lies at the bottom of a hill known as Angel Mountain. The name is fitting, for angels have played a considerable role in keeping their large brood well and happy, Jane and Bud believe, and in bringing other blessings, too. The wooden cross overlooking their property is a constant reminder of that.

The cross was constructed years ago when several of the Surber youngsters were members of a 4-H Club. For a project, they had to build something that the entire community would enjoy. Since Angel Mountain was directly behind them, the kids decided to make a cross that would be visible from the road as their neighbors drove by. Using a scaffold, Bud helped the kids form the cross out of two huge telephone poles. But it needed something more. "I know!" one of the boys said. "Let's put lights on it, so people can see it at night!"

This was a bit more complicated. But since Bud was an electrician for Public Service Company of Colorado, he knew how to tap electric power from the house. He built a junction box, made an extension wire and plug, and connected the other end to several long fluorescent tubes, which the children mounted on both poles. The first night they turned it on, the family stared in awe. It was beautiful, glorious, like a huge heavenly star. Their neighbors, and travelers passing on Highway 285, would see it, too. What a wonderful way to announce Christmas!

The Surbers lit the cross each night during that first holiday season, and continued through January. Everyone appreciated it. One morning, Jane walked down to the mailbox and found a note from a long-distance trucker. "I had been contemplating suicide for a while," he wrote, "and then, from a distance, I saw your cross. I followed the light all across the plains, and by the time I got here, I had changed my mind. Your cross gave me the hope I needed to go on."

Jane and Bud were thrilled that the children's project had actually saved a life. But at the end of January, they received a rude awakening. The electric bill arrived, and due to the cross, "it had skyrocketed," Jane recalls. "We knew we couldn't afford to turn the cross on every night anymore, so we decided to save it for special occasions." And so they did. Whenever they lighted it, travelers who were lost or experiencing car trouble invariably turned in at their gates. "I guess they figured any family with a lighted cross on their property would be willing to help them out," Jane says. "We met a lot of nice people that way."

Years passed. Some of the children married and moved to other areas. Bud was transferred, too. His mother still lived on the ranch—it had been in his family for more than one hundred years—but he, Jane, and the remaining children left Salida. By this time, the cross had fallen into disrepair and hadn't been turned on for several years. Lightning had struck it more than once, and the little connectors between the fluorescent tubes had cracked and rusted, breaking the flow of power. Bud never considered dismantling the cross—he still remembered the care and love the children had put into it. But obviously, its importance had come to an end.

In 1989, Bud retired, and he, Jane, their two youngest sons, and four foster daughters returned to the ranch. Shortly afterward, one of their sons-in-law died suddenly. "It was a tragic time, especially for our widowed daughter, Gail, and her children," Jane says. Gail and her children moved back to the ranch, where the family wrapped them in love and support. But Christmas was fast approaching. How would they get through it this year?

December 24 dawned, and children, in-laws, and grandchildren began to arrive, presents in tow. Despite the laughter and camaraderie, everyone was uncomfortably aware of Gail's pain. If only they could do something special for her, something to make this Christmas a little more bearable! But what?

Jane knew their feelings, and felt the same way. "Gail," she asked as the others milled around the kitchen, making breakfast, mixing cookie dough, and planning their day together. "Is there anything any of us can do for you?"

Gail paused. "I wish . . ."

"Yes?" The kitchen suddenly became very quiet.

"I wish we could light the cross tonight."

Her siblings looked at each other, then at Bud. The cross. Everyone knew it had completely deteriorated. It had been years since they had even thought about it, much less checked to see if it could be restored. Worse, the weather was bitterly cold, with a terrible mountain wind that would make outdoor work even harsher than usual.

But love, real love, never counts the cost. Immediately, everyone reached for jackets and scarves, united in a common cause. If a lighted cross would bring memories of an earlier, happier time to Gail, if it would heal her even for a moment, it was worth trying.

"Our kids, in-law kids, and foster daughters labored outside all day," Jane recalls. Some climbed the high crossbar; others attempted, with frozen fingers, to coax rusted parts to function. Nothing worked.

Jane couldn't see much from the kitchen, but as hours passed with no triumphant shouts, she began to worry. In late afternoon she noticed, with a sinking heart, that snow had begun to fall. Soon, darkness descended, and a son stomped in to get some flashlights. "Anything happening?" Jane asked him.

He looked at her through iced eyelashes, his face raw from the wind. "It's impossible, Mom," he said, slamming the door behind him.

Another hour passed. Finally, Jane threw on a coat and went outside. She could see flashlight beams still moving on the hill, but the cross remained dark. Bud was walking slowly toward the house, and she ran to meet him. "No chance?" she asked quietly.

"None." He sighed and put a numb arm around her. "As soon as one wire's repaired, we find another broken one. There's no end to it. It would take a miracle to help us now."

A miracle. Jane knew that a miracle was what Gail needed, and what her family was feverishly working to give her. Not just a lighted cross, but a sign that she would survive this terrible loss and that life would be good again someday. And weren't miracles what Christmas was all about? "Lord Jesus, send us a miracle," Jane prayed. "Show us your love in a special way tonight."

They had reached the house and now, heartsick and frustrated, Bud moved away from Jane. He looked for a moment at the junction that linked the cross's useless wires to the power source. And then, with one booted foot, he kicked it.

A huge cheer suddenly erupted from the hill. Jane turned first. "Bud, look!" The cross was shining bright.

It was a good Christmas that year, despite the underlying grief. And Gail, perhaps, was the most hopeful of all. God had sent her a message through her family that she was surrounded with love and that he would never abandon her. Although she didn't yet know *how* she would manage, the answers would surely come. The family, too, was joyful. They had sacrificed their comfort for what seemed a desperate cause, and God had rewarded their efforts.

The cross continued to glow each night, a beacon not only for the Surbers but also for everyone traveling along the highway. And it could burn forever, as far as Jane was concerned; a huge electric surcharge would be a small price to pay for the memory of that renewed hope in her daughter's eyes. But it wasn't until the January bill came that Jane realized the full extent of their Christmas gift. For, despite the constant use of extra power, there was no change at all in the bill. It was the same amount due as always. "How could this be?" she asked Bud.

He didn't know. Nor had he been able to figure out just why the cross was turning on automatically each evening. For, despite his kick to the junction box that Christmas Eve, several of the connectors on the poles were still broken. And he had just discovered that the timer he had installed after Christmas had split in two because of the frost. There was no way that electricity could be reaching that cross.

But if you're ever on Colorado's Highway 285 and you pass a cross glowing brightly on Angel Mountain, you might want to stop for just a moment or two. Surely there are miracles there, as in all places that God has touched. And you might even hear the echo of those long-ago heavenly hosts singing the same marvelous message:

"Glory to God in the highest
and on earth peace to those on whom his favor rests."
(Luke 2:14)

What a blessing. For then, for now, forever.

NOTES

1. Keao Mai died recently of cystic fibrosis, a disease she courageously battled for several years. As a coworker says, "She leaves behind an adorable four-year-old daughter, a loving family, countless friends and coworkers, and an empty chair at the dispatch station." And numerous strangers who owe their lives to 'K'.

2. Bonnie told me this story at my book-signing table after I had given a talk on angels. There were a lot of people milling about, and I neglected to get her name. Perhaps she will read this and contact me.

3. A few Christmases after he brought toys to the Thills, Tom Daly became ill. Only a double transplant—liver and kidney—could save him, and there was no donor to be found. On a cold January day, Tom's physician informed the family that unless a miracle donor emerged, Tom would not last through the night. They gathered around his bedside to prepare for the final parting.

   To their astonishment, before the day ended, a miracle donor—a perfect match in both liver and kidney—became available. Tom was rushed into surgery, returned to work in two months, and enjoys a healthy, fulfilling life today

"My wife has always believed that someone brought a blessing to me because I brought blessings to the Thills and others," he says. "'Bread upon the waters' is more than just a nice idea. It works."

4. This book is *The Christmas Menorahs: How A Town Fought Hate* by Janice Cohn, published in 1995 by Albert Whitman and Company in Morton Grove, IL.

DISCUSSION QUESTIONS

1. After reading this book, has your impression of angels changed? How would you have defined them then? What about today?

2. Are angels necessary as intercessors? Can't we just communicate with God?

3. Why do you think angels work so anonymously? Do you think you have ever met an angel?

4. In "The Welcome Visitor," Dr. Clyta Harris was struggling with major life dilemmas. Do you think it was impractical or odd for her to pray for something as benign as ridding her house of mice? Is God really concerned with our "little problems?"

5. In "Marlene's Ministry," Marlene JuHaros asks God for amazing answers, even depending on him to provide dinner for all her boarders. Do you think we limit ourselves by not praying for "big miracles" when we need them? Should we be as daring as Marlene?

6. Have you ever wondered why God sends angels to rescue some people but not others? Have you ever been angry that he didn't rescue you?

7. Suzan King was worried about her teenager's dating choices in "A Mother's Job." instead of trying to manipulate the situation, she gave control over her daughter to God and his Angels. Can you point out various moments in this story when angels might have been involved?

8. Do you think that both angels and saints were helping the Kogovseks in "Angels at the mall?" If so, why? How can we tell the difference between these different but blessed beings?

9. In "The Least of These," several young children apparently communicated with heaven. Do you believe that children are closer to God than most of us? If so, why?

10. What was your favorite story in this book? Your least favorite? Why?

Author's Afterword

I am always interested in hearing from readers who would like to share their angel encounters, miracles, answers to prayer, and other heavenly wonders. Please write to me at PO Box 127, Prospect Heights, Illinois, 60070 or visit my Web site at http://www.joanwanderson.com.

If I can use your story in my future writing, I will contact you for permission.

Joan Wester Anderson

joan@joanwanderson.com

Join In. Speak Up. Help Out!

Would you like to help yourself and the greater Catholic community by simply talking about Catholic life and faith? Would you like to help Loyola Press improve our publications? Would you be willing to share your thoughts and opinions with us in return for rewards and prizes? If so, please consider becoming one of our **special Loyola Press Advisors.**

Loyola Press Advisors is a unique online community of people willing to share with us their perspectives about Catholic life, spirituality, and faith. From time to time, registered advisors are invited to participate in brief online surveys and discussion groups. As a show of our gratitude for their service, we recognize advisors' time and efforts with **gift certificates, cash, and other prizes.** Membership is free and easy. We invite you, and readers like yourself, to join us by registering at www.SpiritedTalk.org.

Your personal information gathered by SpiritedTalk.org is stored in a protected, **confidential** database. Your information will never be sold to or shared with another third party! And SpiritedTalk.org is for research purposes only; at no time will we use the Web site or your membership to try to sell you anything.

Once you have registered at SpiritedTalk.org, every now and then you will be invited to participate in surveys—most take less than ten minutes to complete. Survey topics include your thoughts and ideas regarding the products and services you use in relation to Catholic life and spiritual growth. You may also have the opportunity to evaluate new Loyola Press products and services before they are released for sale. For each survey you complete, you will earn gift certificates, points, or prizes! Membership is voluntary; you may opt out at any time.

Please consider this opportunity to help Loyola Press improve our products and better serve you and the greater Catholic community. We invite you to visit **www.SpiritedTalk.org,** take a look, and register today!

The Power of Miracles
True Stories of God's Presence

In the Arms of Angels
True Stories of Heavenly Guardians

Joan Wester Anderson

The Power of Miracles, ISBN 0-8294-2213-7, 252 pages • $14.95
7⁵/₁₆" x 7⁷/₁₆" Paperback

In the Arms of Angels, ISBN 0-8294-2040-1, 292 pages • $14.95
7⁵/₁₆" x 7⁷/₁₆" Paperback

∞ In *The Power of Miracles,* Anderson brings together her most glorious and remarkable accounts—stories of mysterious rescues, celestial visions, unexpected healings, inexplicable protection, and many other signs and wonders.

∞ *In the Arms of Angels* brings together some of the most compelling true stories of angelic appearances in the lives of ordinary people. These wonderful and extraordinary accounts light up the pages, bringing comfort and renewed faith to everyone who reads them.

LOYOLAPRESS.

phone: 800.621.1008 fax: 773.281.0555 visit: www.LoyolaBooks.org